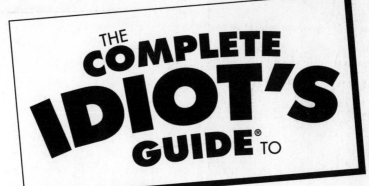

THE COMPLETE IDIOT'S GUIDE® TO

Wine and Food Pairing

D1040462

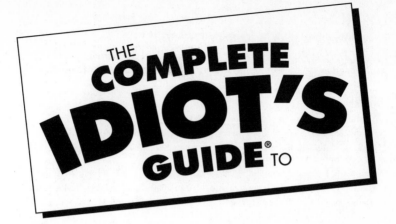

Wine and Food Pairing

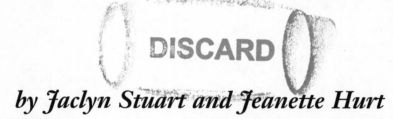

DISCARD

by Jaclyn Stuart and Jeanette Hurt

ALPHA

A member of Penguin Group (USA) Inc.

To my family and friends; especially Eric, Dad, Mom, and Nick.—Jaclyn
To my family, especially to my father, who loves drinking Shiraz with everything; and my mother, who enjoys drinking other wines with food.—Jeanette

ALPHA BOOKS

Published by the Penguin Group

Penguin Group (USA) Inc., 375 Hudson Street, New York, New York 10014, USA

Penguin Group (Canada), 90 Eglinton Avenue East, Suite 700, Toronto, Ontario M4P 2Y3, Canada (a division of Pearson Penguin Canada Inc.)

Penguin Books Ltd., 80 Strand, London WC2R 0RL, England

Penguin Ireland, 25 St. Stephen's Green, Dublin 2, Ireland (a division of Penguin Books Ltd.)

Penguin Group (Australia), 250 Camberwell Road, Camberwell, Victoria 3124, Australia (a division of Pearson Australia Group Pty. Ltd.)

Penguin Books India Pvt. Ltd., 11 Community Centre, Panchsheel Park, New Delhi—110 017, India

Penguin Group (NZ), 67 Apollo Drive, Rosedale, North Shore, Auckland 1311, New Zealand (a division of Pearson New Zealand Ltd.)

Penguin Books (South Africa) (Pty.) Ltd., 24 Sturdee Avenue, Rosebank, Johannesburg 2196, South Africa

Penguin Books Ltd., Registered Offices: 80 Strand, London WC2R 0RL, England

Copyright © 2010 by Jeanette Hurt

International Standard Book Number: 978-1-61564-015-7
Library of Congress Catalog Card Number: 2009941616

12 11 10   8 7 6 5 4 3 2 1

Interpretation of the printing code: The rightmost number of the first series of numbers is the year of the book's printing; the rightmost number of the second series of numbers is the number of the book's printing. For example, a printing code of 10-1 shows that the first printing occurred in 2010.

Printed in the United States of America

Note: This publication contains the opinions and ideas of its authors. It is intended to provide helpful and informative material on the subject matter covered. It is sold with the understanding that the authors and publisher are not engaged in rendering professional services in the book. If the reader requires personal assistance or advice, a competent professional should be consulted.

The authors and publisher specifically disclaim any responsibility for any liability, loss, or risk, personal or otherwise, which is incurred as a consequence, directly or indirectly, of the use and application of any of the contents of this book.

Most Alpha books are available at special quantity discounts for bulk purchases for sales promotions, premiums, fund-raising, or educational use. Special books, or book excerpts, can also be created to fit specific needs.

For details, write: Special Markets, Alpha Books, 375 Hudson Street, New York, NY 10014.

Publisher: *Marie Butler-Knight*
Associate Publisher: *Mike Sanders*
Senior Managing Editor: *Billy Fields*
Executive Editor: *Randy Ladenheim-Gil*
Development Editor: *Jennifer Moore*
Senior Production Editor: *Megan Douglass*

Copy Editor: *Monica Stone*
Cover Designer: *Kurt Owens*
Book Designer: *Trina Wurst*
Indexer: *Johnna Vanhoose Dinse*
Layout: *Ayanna Lacey*
Proofreader: *Laura Caddell*

Contents at a Glance

Appendixes

Contents

Introduction

Wine and food pairings seem to be everywhere these days. Restaurants are hosting more wine dinners than ever before, and they are even listing pairing suggestions on their standard menus. Once solely the domain of five-star restaurants, even mom and pop cafés and national chains are getting into the game. Community colleges, restaurants, and wine stores are offering special classes on pairing wine with food. There's no doubt about it: our interest in pairing wine with food is here to stay!

Even though wine and food pairings are growing in popularity, they're still more than a bit mystifying. At times they can be downright intimidating, especially when you try to create a perfect pairing experience at home.

It's okay to feel a little intimidated by the thought of selecting a wine that brings out the best qualities of a food. We both were more than a little skittish when we started matching wines and foods, and we work with wine and food for a living! But once we got over our initial jitters, we discovered that pairing up wine and food can be really fun and, once you understand the basics, it's really not that hard at all.

Wine and food pairing is exciting. There's nothing more satisfying than pulling together a great meal and matching it with great wines. The wines bring out flavors in the foods, and the foods bring out aromas in the wines, and together, they're a more satisfying culinary experience than they would be on their own. In fact, when wine and food are paired perfectly, it can be a downright heavenly experience. Each bite, each sip, tastes more perfect than the last.

We hope you'll discover the same sense of excitement and enjoyment in pairings in this book. *The Complete Idiot's Guide to Wine and Food Pairing* will have you matching wines and foods together like a pro. By the end of this book, you'll be able to host your own wine dinners, and you'll also be able to pick wines off restaurant menus with panache. Happy pairing!

How to Use This Book

Part 1, "How to Taste," covers food and wine-tasting basics and offers a brief history of wine and food pairings. You will learn proper serving etiquette and find out what tools you need to enhance your tasting experience of both wine and food.

Part 2, "Breaking It Down: Pairing Basics," gives you the basic concepts you'll need to pair white, red, sparkling, and dessert wines. It also teaches you how to match up ingredients and sauces with wines, and provides you with suggested pairings for dozens of wines and foods.

Part 3, "Putting It Back Together: Pairing Principles," applies the concepts you learned in Part 2 and introduces you to other pairing techniques, including drawing on some measurable characteristics of wine and using your intuition as a guide. Additionally, you'll learn how to experiment with pairing new wines and foods and match many types of "ethnic" cuisines with wine.

Part 4, "Pairing Experiences," shows you how to order wine to match your food selections in restaurants, how to shop for wine, and throw a pairings party. It will even reveal to you how to apply pairing principles to other beverages.

Extras

We have to admit: we're wine geeks, and we dearly love to share our knowledge and spread our enthusiasm to anyone who cares to pay attention. For your special benefit (and because we couldn't help ourselves!), we've added many sip-sized pairing tidbits to each chapter, which you'll find under the following headings:

> **Perfect Pairings**
> The hints and tips in these boxes will make you a pairing pro in no time.

> **def•i•ni•tion**
> Turn to these boxes for definitions of out-of-the-ordinary wine and culinary terms.

Corked

Turn to these boxes for tips on how to identify and avoid pairing snafus.

Wine Nerd

Oenophiles, rejoice! These trivia-filled boxes are for folks who like to read the back labels of wine bottles.

Acknowledgments

We couldn't have written this book without the loving support of our husbands, families, and friends. We also owe a round of applause to Alterra Coffee's Alterra at the Lake Café—their aromatic brews— paired with their delicious pastries and sandwiches—kept us energized as we drafted the manuscript. Thanks also goes out to Damon Brown, Jeanette's writing buddy; Marilyn Allen, our knowledgeable agent; our wonderful acquisitions editor, Randy Ladenheim-Gil; our equally fantastic development editor, Jennifer Moore; and our stellar production editor Megan Douglass; and the other talented people at Alpha Books.

Trademarks

All terms mentioned in this book that are known to be, or are suspected of being, trademarks or service marks have been appropriately capitalized. Alpha Books and Penguin Group (USA) Inc. cannot attest to the accuracy of this information. Use of a term in this book should not be regarded as affecting the validity of any trademark or service mark.

Part 1

How to Taste

This first part serves as your appetizer, whetting your appetite for the pairing experiences you'll encounter in subsequent parts of the book. You'll get a taste of the history of food and wine pairings as well as a tutorial in tasting wine. Wine and food, when paired properly, are capable of transcending the simple acts of drinking and eating. You will learn how to enhance the experience by using appropriate glasses and serving your wine properly.

Wine and Food Pairing 101

In This Chapter

- ◆ Three basic pairing outcomes
- ◆ It all comes down to personal preference
- ◆ A brief history of pairings
- ◆ The modern wine dinner

Nothing tastes quite so sublime as when wine and food are perfectly matched. Conversely, nothing tastes quite so awful as wine and food that clash. A perfectly seared pork tenderloin served with a glass of dry rosé elevates a simple meal and turns it into a heavenly tasting experience, whereas a grilled ribeye served with a glass of oaky Chardonnay ruins a perfectly good steak and a perfectly good glass of wine, proving that two rights can sometimes make a wrong.

With wine dinners becoming popular everywhere from New York to New Mexico, diners are getting a taste of sublime, perfect pairs more frequently than ever. Still, even with such growing popularity, wine and food pairing can be a mysterious and intimidating endeavor. The unfortunate result is that some of us just head blindly into our local wine shops or liquor stores and heed whatever advice the clerk behind the counter dishes out, be it good or bad.

But the process of pairing doesn't have to be difficult. Like Toto in the *Wizard of Oz*, the aim of this book is to pull back the curtain and reveal the man wearing the wizard's mask. Selecting a bottle of wine to go with your meal should be a fun, engaging project—akin to trying a new cuisine or learning a new hobby.

This chapter introduces you to the basic outcomes of wine and food matchups. You'll also get a brief history of pairings leading up to the modern wine dinner.

The Big Three: Wine and Food Pairing Outcomes

Wine and food are like Laverne and Shirley, or George Burns and Gracie Allen, or even Hall and Oates. But like celebrity duos, not all wine and food pairings are successful. Whether you plan your pairings or just match them up blindly, you will achieve one of the following three basic outcomes every single time you bring both of them to the table:

◆ The wine will overpower the food.

◆ The food will overpower the wine.

◆ The wine and the food will enhance one another.

The first two concepts are easy to recognize when you experience them. You're enjoying a good glass of wine or a nice bite of food, but when you bring the wine and food together in your mouth, it takes every ounce of good manners not to spit them out. Instead of a symphony of flavors, a cacophony of clashing tastes converge on your tongue. Something in the wine and food just doesn't work together.

You know that the problem isn't with the wine or with the food because when you tasted them each individually, their flavors were just fine.

The wine was neither *corked* nor *oxidized*, and the food wasn't spoiled or poorly prepared. The problem occurs only when you taste them together. The food is doing the tango while the wine is trying to waltz, and in the process, they're tying up your tongue's taste buds.

def•i•ni•tion

Corked wine has been exposed to bad bacteria that has spoiled the wine, making it smell and taste like wet cardboard.

Oxidized wine, oft confused with corked wine, is when too much air has made the wine go stale, causing it to smell like Sherry or vinegar. This can happen to a bottle of wine if you leave it uncorked overnight, for example. It can also occur to wine that has been incorrectly bottled or stored, and it happens to wine in all price ranges.

One reason for this tasting malfunction is either the wine is overpowering the food or the food is overpowering the wine. For instance, if you paired a strong wine with a more delicate food, chances are the wine is the culprit. If you served a strong-flavored or spicy food then, most likely, it's the food that has quashed the wine. A Cabernet Sauvignon will completely overpower broiled fish, for example, while a spicy bowl of chili will drown out the flavors of a delicate Pinot Gris.

Another reason this occurs is, perhaps, because you simply misjudged the actual flavors of the wine and/or the food. This happened to Jeanette once when she was serving an expensive bottle of Sauvignon Blanc and one of her favorite goat cheeses. Cloudy Bay, a fruity and refreshing New Zealand Sauvignon Blanc, did nothing to enhance the creamy Humboldt Fog, an ash-coated California goat cheese.

While Sauvignon Blancs typically go well with most chèvres (goat cheeses), this citrusy white clashed with this unctuous and earthy, sweet goat's milk cheese. Jeanette

Perfect Pairings

All too often people fail to appreciate the varying characteristics of wines, assuming that all reds and all whites are similar. But whereas a fresh, young red wine, like Beaujolais Nouveau, would be overpowered by a peppercorn-garlic-blue-cheese-encrusted sirloin; a peppery red, such as Shiraz will bind beautifully with the steak's strong flavors.

could have avoided this clash—which she describes as "fingernails scratching across the blackboard of her taste buds"—had she followed one basic rule about pairings: avoid making assumptions. Not all wine varietals are the same.

A French Chardonnay is very different from a California Chardonnay. How, where, and what year a wine was made, can all affect its taste. And that doesn't even get into the distinctions each winemaker brings to his or her wines. The same can be said for flavors of foods—how something is prepared, what sauces and accompaniments are served with it, and where it comes from, can all affect its taste.

> **Corked**
>
> When it comes to specific wine varietals, don't make assumptions. Always double-check a wine's flavor profile—with the label description as well as with the wine seller or sommelier. Sometimes a perfect pairing turns out to be perfectly awful, while a not-so-obvious pairing can turn out to be heavenly.

Now, that brings us to another important point. When you go in search of a perfect pairing, you will make mistakes, and that's okay. Professional sommeliers and chefs sometimes taste 20 different wines with one dish, or 20 different dishes with one wine to come up with what they consider to be a perfect pairing. So cut yourself some slack.

By being adventurous enough to try new things, you will come across some do-not-ever-pair-again matchups, but you will also stumble upon some gems. And those gems are what food and wine pairing is all about.

> **def·i·ni·tion**
>
> **Oenophile** is just a fancy way of saying "wine lover."

It is this desire for a perfect pair—when the wine and the food dance together in perfect harmony in your mouth—that drives us *oenophiles* and foodies. Which brings us to a third potential outcome of pairings.

When the wine and the food enhance each other, they sometimes bring out almost a third and separate flavor profile. They taste good on their own, but together, they create a third, distinctive taste that makes you swoon, that elevates the entire tasting experience. You go, "A-ha! This is what wine and food pairing is all about." This can happen when you take a peppercorn-encrusted steak and pair it with a peppery Shiraz. Or when you take a sweet, dessert wine and match it up with blue cheese drizzled with honey.

Jaclyn experienced this when she tasted Pinot Noir paired with seared ahi tuna for the first time. "It made me realize the potential of pairings," she says. While these are examples of clear-as-crystal pairings, not all perfect pairings are, well, that perfect.

Sometimes a pairing is just okay. That brings us to another point about pairings: personal preferences.

Personal Preferences and Pairings: Degrees of Perfection

Some wine writers and oenophiles say that most foods and wines can react indifferently to each other. Instead of creating culinary fireworks—of the good or bad kind—they exist in a blah-blah neverwhere. They're next to each other, they're experienced together, but they really don't touch each other or interact with each other at all. They don't bring out each other's worst characteristics, but they don't really enhance each other either. They're as neutral as distilled water.

Except that they're not. There are degrees of pairing perfection. A good pairing might be spot-on, but sometimes it is just okay. A bad pairing might be spit inducing, but often, it's just—eh—not so good. What makes a pairing good or bad, sometimes, is simply a matter of personal opinion.

That able *sommelier* might love Shiraz with her veal, but you might really prefer Pinot Noir. And you can't really say that either of you are right or wrong. Pairings are like food and wine preferences, they're a matter of personal taste.

def•i•ni•tion

A **sommelier** is a wine professional, usually a restaurant employee, who has earned a certification in wine studies and service and who is in charge of all things wine, especially creating wine and food pairings.

When Jaclyn arranges classes to illustrate the concept of food and wine pairings, she often selects a wine that she thinks will pair perfectly with a selected dish, another wine that is just okay with the dish, and a third that is downright awful with the dish.

Invariably, a small percentage of the tasters somehow adore that third pairing. They don't just like it, they rave about it. The first few times Jaclyn observed this phenomenon, she thought she had made a mistake, so she'd go back and taste that third wine with the dish again. "After tasting it, I could see what they were picking up, and why they liked it. There was a nuance that I hadn't picked up on," she says.

While she understood their adoration, Jaclyn didn't revise her own opinion. But she also learned how varied people's taste buds and preferences are. In the end, sometimes, it's just about what you like.

A Little Bit about History

Wine and food go way back together. In fact, wines and other fermented beverages are probably some of the very first, consumable liquids humankind ever developed. If you study archaeological ruins of the earliest civilizations, many of them have wine-related relics. The ancient Greeks kept wine around the house in clay pots. Noah packed some bottles on the Ark. (The Bible, in fact, has numerous references to wine.) Shakespeare, Roman philosophers, and even Egyptian hieroglyphics, all mention wine.

> **Wine Nerd**
>
> "Nothing more excellent or valuable than wine was ever granted by the gods to man."
> —Plato

Most early references don't specifically talk about wine and food being paired together, but it's pretty obvious that they were consumed jointly.

In many cultures, wines and local cuisines developed together, side-by-side. Since they "grew up" together, they usually taste good together. For example, Chianti is almost a foregone choice to pair with Tuscan cuisine. And don't ever think about serving beef bourguignon without a French Burgundy. This is called pairing by *terroir*, and is fully explored in Chapter 10.

Over time, though, wine grapes have expanded beyond their original terroirs. While newer wine regions do sometimes match the local cuisines, they often don't have the centuries of history and development that European matches typically do.

Also, wines are now being served with foods that traditionally were never paired with wines. Which brings us to the modern concept of wine and food pairing.

The Modern Wine Dinner Phenomenon

Ah, modern wine dinners. While Old World winemakers have served some of their wines with certain dishes for centuries, in the past 10 years the modern wine dinner has taken wine and food pairings to a whole new level. These modern meals are orchestrated with great care by chefs, winemakers, and sommeliers, almost as if they are a symphony of eating and drinking.

At some restaurants, chefs and sommeliers meet late into the night planning special dishes and wine selections for their daily menus. Other restaurants may rely on a wine-savvy staff to make spontaneous pairing recommendations. Food and wine pairings, which were once exclusive to five-star restaurants serving gourmet fare, are becoming increasingly common in run-of-the-mill restaurants. Even chain restaurants, such as the Olive Garden, offer wine-pairing suggestions on their menus. But the modern wine dinner goes far beyond restaurants.

The modern wine dinner evolved as the California wine industry grew. Many West Coast wineries started hosting dinners to showcase their wines, and some even added restaurants to their wine-making facilities solely to highlight their wines.

Around the same time, notable chefs on both coasts began hosting wine dinners. Often these dinners featured a winemaker who happened to be in the area promoting his or her wines. More and more wineries discovered that wine dinners were a great way to introduce new customers to their wines. Now winemakers energetically visit restaurants around the country to host these dinners.

These culinary events spurred an increasing interest in wine lists—especially wine-by-the-glass menus at restaurants—and people's appetite for wine began to grow. Add to this mix an increasing interest in food as evidenced by the Food Network's phenomenal growth and the *locavore* movement.

def•i•ni•tion

A **locavore** is someone who embraces, and tries to eat, local foods, often grown within a 100-mile radius of his or her home. The local food movement or locavore movement started in California, not far from Sonoma County's wine country.

Wine Nerd

While today's chefs daringly pair wine with everything from curry to cockles, in the past not all food was thought worthy of an accompanying wine. A 1976 book, *Entertaining with Wine*, adamantly advises against pairing wine with curry. It also expresses horror at the thought of serving wine with salad.

The Least You Need to Know

- ◆ Wine and food pairings have three outcomes: the wine overpowers the food, the food overpowers the wine, or the wine and food enhance each other.

- ◆ Personal preference plays a large part in determining pairing perfection.

- ◆ There are degrees of perfection in pairings.

- ◆ Historically, wines and culinary traditions have grown-up together, which is why French wines pair beautifully with many French foods.

- ◆ The popularity of the modern wine dinner developed concurrently with a burgeoning interest in gourmet foods and wine in general.

2

Tasting Basics

In This Chapter

- How to taste wine
- How to taste food
- How to dissect a dish
- The main aromas of wine

Everyone knows how to taste. Just chug down a little wine or chow down a little food, and you're good to go, right? But even though you've been eating and drinking all of your life, there is a distinct difference, when you pay close attention. By taking the time to discern aromas, flavors, and textures, you elevate the experience of eating and drinking beyond the mundane.

There's an art to tasting—truly tasting—wine and food. This chapter will give you the basics for tasting both. Once you truly understand how to taste each individually, you'll be able to taste, and pair the two together, successfully.

The Eight S's of Wine Tasting

In fancy restaurants, you might see people jiggling their wine glasses and then gargling their wine. Really. They're not doing it to be pretentious—or at least most of them aren't. Instead, they're just trying to properly savor their drink. To really get the most out of your wine, you need to study its nuances and identify its *aromas*.

def•i•ni•tion

Aromas are, simply put, the smells or scents of a certain grape when made into wine. It's what wine smells like. Aromas are to wine what flavors are to food, and you need to identify them in order to match them up successfully with food flavors.

A good way to identify and enjoy these aromas, and thus truly taste wine, is to follow Jaclyn's system, "The Eight S's of Wine Tasting: see, swirl, sniff, sip, slurp, swish, swallow, and savor." This approach brings out the nuances of different wines, providing you with information you will need to pair wine with food.

Corked

Just because a wine has a certain aroma doesn't mean it actually has that particular substance in it. For instance, a wine that has an aroma of pear, smells like a pear, but doesn't actually have pears in it. It's the same as when someone says a type of meat tastes like chicken when there isn't actually chicken in it.

Here's the basic procedure:

See. Look at the wine. Note its color, hold it up to the light to see its clarity. If it is sparkling, notice the size and arrangement of its bubbles. No matter what kind of wine it is, it should be clear, not cloudy or murky.

Swirl. Gently holding the stem of your glass between your thumb and forefinger, rotate it a few times to swirl the wine around. You don't have to create a violent, centrifugal force in your glass—just an easy rotation. This will release the aromas of the wine for the next step, and the wine will coat the inside of the glass, creating a little veil that may streak downward. These teardrops or streaks are known as "legs," and their color and how fast they drip down the glass can reveal the wine's age or alcohol content.

Sniff. Really stick your nose in the glass and take a deep breath. This is where the tasting actually begins since so much of your taste is affected by your sense of smell. In fact, if you part your lips just slightly while inhaling, you will actually draw the aromas of wine onto your palate, which will help you distinguish the "nose" of the wine. What does the wine smell like? Cherries? Apricots? Your sixth grade homeroom? At this point, a sommelier or an experienced oenophile can usually predict how the wine will taste.

Sip. Now, take a sip—just a little one. You want just enough to coat your palate. Any more than that will force you to swallow it before you can complete the rest of the tasting process.

Slurp. Go ahead. It's not rude. Slurping aerates the wine further, and it also involves your sense of smell in the tasting process.

Swish. Move the wine across your tongue and throughout your mouth. Your different taste buds—sweet, sour, salty, bitter—are located on varying parts of your tongue, so you want to make sure your entire tongue gets to taste the wine. It's not necessary to gargle the wine, but do let it really envelop your mouth. At this point, some people suggest "chewing" your wine, or to drink it as if you were eating something solid.

> **Wine Nerd**
>
> A lot of taste involves your nose, as anyone who has a stuffy head cold can attest. When you can't smell, you can't taste.

Swallow. Let the wine gently leave your mouth, guided by your esophagus, down to your stomach. Notice if there are any aftertastes or lingering aromas, often referred to as the wine's "finish." Usually the longer and more pleasurable the finish, the higher quality the wine.

Savor. Sit, think, and take in the wine. Does it taste the way it smells? Does it taste differently from its aroma? How would you describe its flavor? Does the flavor have a long finish or a short one? Was it balanced? What do its flavors and aromas remind you of? Most importantly, did you like it? Why, or why not?

With practice you will be able to perform all eight steps within a few moments. And you can use these same steps to taste beer, liquors, teas, and even juices. But with beer, like with sparkling wine, go easy on the swirling to release aromas. Too much swirling and the bubbles might get swished out.

The Six N's of Food Tasting

Food tasting involves a similar method, which we call, "The Six N's: notice, nose, knead, nibble, nosh, and enjoy." This method of tasting food is modeled on the way judges at certain juried food contests taste food.

Here's our recommended method:

Notice. Really look at the food. What color is it? Is it visually appealing? Why or why not?

Nose. Sniff it. Inhale its aromas. What does it smell like? Is there one predominant scent, like an herb, or are there competing scents? Does it smell like it's supposed to smell like? For example, if it's a beef roast, does it smell beefy?

kNead. Touch your food. If you are in a restaurant or polite company, use your fork to do this. Gently press on it. What kind of texture does it have? Is it soft or firm? Smooth or chunky?

Nibble. Take a tiny bite. What does it taste like? Is its taste stronger or less pronounced than its aroma? Does its taste match your expectations?

Nosh. Really move the food around your mouth. Smooth it over your tongue, and let its flavors coat your mouth, covering your tongue completely so that you can pick up all four tastes—sweet, salty, bitter, sour—as well as any *umami* flavor. What is the intensity of its flavor? What is the texture like?

eNjoy. Swallow and really savor the food. Note the flavor and length of the finish. Does it have an aftertaste? How did its taste and aroma fill your mouth? Did it have a bite to it? Again, most importantly, did you like it? Why, or why not?

def•i•ni•tion

def•i•ni•tion

Umami, a Japanese word that means savory, is often referred to as the fifth taste. Umami often rounds out other tastes and sometimes can be hard to pick up by itself. Some people describe it as "meaty," and its flavor can be found in meats, mushrooms, and in the chemical form of MSG. Umami can also be tasted in more complex foods like Parmigiano-Reggiano, Thai fish sauce, and Worcestershire sauce.

Dissecting a Dish

Sometimes, we eat simply—slices of fresh red pepper; a crisp, Granny Smith apple; just a piece of poached chicken. But more often we eat more complex dishes. The food we consume is often a combination of ingredients. Most of the time when we pair wine with food, we are pairing with complex dishes or entire courses. Rather than simply apples, you're dealing with apples in a tart topped with whipped cream. Instead of plain chicken, you've got sweet and sour chicken served over brown rice with a side of stir-fried veggies.

To pair such complex dishes, you first have to break them down into their various flavor components. Start by looking at the whole dish, then dissect it into its predominant flavors. To understand how to do this, let's go through it with a simple Italian dish—beef ravioli topped with tomato sauce.

First of all, identify its main ingredients: pasta, basil, oregano, garlic, beef, tomato sauce, and maybe a sprinkling of grated Parmigiano-Reggiano cheese.

Of these ingredients, what are their respective flavors, and then, of this dish, what flavor overpowers all of the other ingredients? Unless it is an exceedingly beefy filling and the sauce is skimpy, chances are the primary taste sensation going on in your mouth is tomato. The sweetness and the tartness of the tomato, are the overriding flavors.

That is the flavor you're going to match with wine. Therefore, instead of pouring a heavy Cabernet Sauvignon because it is a beef dish, you will want a lighter red—a Sangiovese or a Tempranillo, perhaps— something that goes with the tomato taste.

You must also consider whether you are pairing the wine to go with the food or whether you are pairing the food to go with the wine.

The difference between pairing the wine with the food, or pairing the food with the wine, is subtle but important. The starting point—the food or the wine—will determine how you go about the pairing.

Let's say you are celebrating your anniversary with your spouse. Perhaps to commemorate the event, you decide to make a rack of lamb. Or maybe you decide to mark the occasion by uncorking a special bottle of wine that you brought back from your honeymoon to France.

> **Perfect Pairings**
>
> Pair the wine to the dish, or pair the dish to the wine? The difference in the goal of the pairing will make all the difference in the outcome of the pairing itself.

If you are starting with the bottle of wine, you'll first identify the aromas and characteristics of the wine, then you will look to prepare a dish that has corresponding flavors. If you are starting with a dish, then you'll dissect the dish into flavors and look for a wine that has aromas to match it.

Aromatic Aromas

What flavors are to food, aromas are to wine. While we involve both our senses of smell and taste when eating food and drinking wine, taste is more predominant in eating, and smell is more predominant in drinking. This is one reason why wine and food pairings create a complete sensory experience.

Most of us grasp the four basic tastes in food—sweet, salty, sour, and bitter. And some of us even have a handle on the fifth taste, umami. But while we understand the basic tastes of food, the basic aromas of wine tend to confuse us.

Smelling wine, like tasting food, is pretty subjective. But just as chefs develop a better palette for food and can identify spices and herbs that some of us might not even be able to identify by name, sommeliers develop a better nose for wine and can recognize aromas that others might miss. Sommeliers have developed their noses by smelling a lot of wines, but they also have trained their noses to pick up different aromas. With a little practice, you can develop a better nose for wine, too.

One of the best ways to practice identifying aromas is to select a handful of wines, and then arrange a dozen or so different foods, flowers, and other aromatic items to sniff while smelling your wines. It's easier, for example, to pick out cherry notes in a Zinfandel when you have a small bowl of cut-up cherries to smell.

> ### Wine Nerd
>
> The Kendall-Jackson Winery in Sonoma County has an extensive wine garden that allows visitors to experience aromatic tastings on their own. The gardens are divided by grape—Pinot Noir, Sauvignon Blanc, etc.— but they aren't rows of grape vines. Instead, each section offers a selection of fruits, vegetables, flowers, and herbs that mimic the aromas of that grape. Visitors are encouraged to take their glasses of wine out into the gardens and pick the plants to taste or smell with the wines.

When Jaclyn taught wine classes to waitstaffs at the restaurants and resorts she worked at, she'd bring along fruits, vegetables, herbs, flowers, and other aromatic ingredients. Then, with the wines she selected, she would have the waitstaff smell both the wines and the ingredients together. She also used this same technique to improve her own nose. "Sauvignon Blancs are often described as having gooseberry aromas, but most people don't know what gooseberries smell like," Jaclyn explains. "When I was in New York City, I stopped at a Whole Foods, and I found some gooseberries. I had to buy them, and yes, they do smell just like many Sauvignon Blancs."

By doing these aromatic tastings, you can feel the impact different flavor combinations have on your total sensory experience. The sommelier at the Lansdowne Resort in Leesburg, Virginia, takes guests into her herb garden, and she demonstrates how a glass of Viognier tastes differently when you enjoy it with pineapple sage than when you enjoy it with rosemary or lemongrass. Aromatic tastings also help you understand a wine's *bouquet*. While many people use the words "aroma" and "bouquet"

def•i•ni•tion

A wine's **bouquet** is the aromas that come from secondary sources, in other words, the barreling and bottling processes.

interchangeably, they are not the same thing. Aromas are the smells of wine, created by the grapes themselves, whereas bouquets come from the process and/or aging of wine. The oaky smell of Chardonnay, for example, doesn't come from Chardonnay grapes—it comes from the barrel, and thus, "oaky" is a bouquet description, not an aroma description. However, don't let this distinction trip you up—they both have to do with how wine smells.

So go ahead and set up your own tastings. Comparative, aromatic tastings are the cheapest and simplest way to help you understand wine's many aromas.

Another option that produces the same results is to purchase a wine aroma kit at a gourmet store or wine shop. These kits, also called wine essence kits or wine bouquet kits, typically offer vials filled with 10 to 30 different scents.

Corked

Wine aroma sets range in price between $75 and $400. Instead of buying a set you'll use once or twice, buy the actual ingredients instead. It is less expensive, and you can cook with the food and use the flowers and plants in a floral arrangement.

To better understand aromas, and the wines in which you are likely to experience them, here is Jaclyn's master list of aromas and bouquets for white and red wines. We encourage you to seek out these various aromatic ingredients and create your own wine aroma tasting.

White Wine

Aromas:

- **Citrus** (most prevalent in cooler climate and younger wines)   lemon, lime, grapefruit, orange, tangerine, kumquat

- **Stone Fruit**   apricot, peach

- **Apple**   green apple, golden apple, red apple, baked apple

- **Tropical Fruit** (most prevalent in warmer climate wines) pineapple, mango, banana, guava, melon, passion fruit

- **Other Fruit**   pear, lychee, fig, green tomato, gooseberry, dried fruits

- **Floral**   rose petal, orange blossom, honeysuckle, "perfume"

- **Herb/Spice**   white pepper, mint, basil, anise, lemongrass, eucalyptus, tea leaf

- **Vegetal**   grass, green pepper, asparagus, green pea

- **Earth** (most prevalent in Old-World wines)   wet stone, chalk, flint, sea salt, metal

Bouquet:

- **Oak**   "baking spice," vanilla, coconut, cinnamon, nutmeg, toast, roasted nuts, butterscotch, pine, buttered popcorn

- **Aging**   honey, beeswax, lanolin, brioche, nuts, petrol/gasoline, gingerbread, butter

Red Wine

Aromas:

- **Cherry** (found in some form in nearly every red wine)   bing cherry, dark cherry, dried cherry, cherry jam

- **Bramble Fruit**   blackberry, raspberry, boysenberry

- **Other Fruit**   plum, black currant, blueberry, cranberry, strawberry, orange peel, blood orange, tomato, dried fruits

- **Floral**   lavender, violet, rose

- **Herb/Spice**   black pepper, white pepper, tobacco, basil, tarragon, anise, bay leaf, mint, cinnamon, eucalyptus, dried herbs, black tea

- **Vegetal** (most prevalent in cool climate wines)   green pepper, beet, plant stalk, olive

- **Earth**   "barnyard," dust, dirt, gravel, flint, pencil lead, mushroom, truffle, "forest floor," saline

Bouquet:

- **Oak**   cocoa, vanilla, "baking spice," coffee, toast, smoke, charcoal, nuts, coconut, caramel, maple syrup, cedar, "cigar box"

- **Aging**   mushroom, leather, bacon, meat/soy sauce, wax

Bad Wine Aromas:

- Wet newspaper, rotten eggs, band-aid, geranium, wet dog, rubber, skunk, raw onion, mold

The aromas in wine and the flavors in food, when paired well together, create a dynamic sensory experience. The food covers your mouth, the wine overwhelms your nose, and together, they create magic. That's why perfect pairings are so pleasurable.

The Least You Need to Know

- The Eight S's of Wine Tasting are: see, swirl, sniff, sip, slurp, swish, swallow, and savor.

- The Six N's of Food Tasting are: notice, nose, kNead, nibble, nosh, and eNjoy.

- To better pair a dish, break it down into its predominant flavors.

- When you plan to pair, either start with the wine or start with the food.

- Aromas are to wine what flavors are to food.

3

Enhancing the Wine-Tasting Experience

In This Chapter

◆ Glassware basics

◆ Understanding decanting

◆ Wine serving temperatures

It goes almost without saying that presentation makes a meal more enjoyable, and the food seems to taste better, simply because we eat with our eyes first. The same can be said about drinking wine; a nice glass makes it a more enjoyable experience.

Whereas the actual taste of the food does not change whether it is served on a fine piece of china or a paper plate, the type of glass used does affect a wine's aromas. In this chapter, you'll learn how to pair your wine with the most appropriate glass. In addition, you will explore the art of decanting, and get the low-down on serving wine at the right temperature. Understanding these wine-tasting practices will help you better enjoy wine, pick out more nuances and aromas in wine, and thus improve your pairing prowess.

A Glass Is Just a Glass ... Or Is It?

Shopping for wine glasses was once a simple experience. It used to be that there were only three types of glasses: white, red, and champagne. If you ordered wine at a mom-and-pop restaurant you might even have found yourself slurping wine out of a tumbler. Nowadays though, you need a chart just to keep all of your options straight.

Go to any notable wine shop to purchase some stemware for your wines, and before you reach the check out line your head will be spinning. Some manufacturers offer more than 50 types of wine glasses, not including design choices.

With so many options, the choice can be downright frustrating. Obviously, mason jars or tumblers are one option, or you could purchase the 50 or so varieties available so that you have the perfect glass for just about every type of wine out there. But there is a middle ground, and though you can purchase special varietal glasses, sticking to the basics is best.

The Four Basic Types of Wine Glasses

Start with four basic types of stemware: white, red, champagne, and dessert. If you don't drink a lot of dessert wine, just go with the first three. When looking at glassware, keep in mind that to enjoy a wine fully you need to have room to swirl and sniff. That means those cutesy, shallow, decorative glasses aren't going to do the trick.

Perfect Pairings

Though it's difficult to fully appreciate the bouquet and aromas of some complex reds in a white wine glass, you can drink red wine in white wine glasses. White wine glasses are the most important set of glasses to start with.

The key is to keep it simple. A basic, white wine glass holds 5 to 6 ounces of wine. If you opt for only one set of glasses, this is the set to get. Although good red wines and champagnes taste better in other glasses, you'll get by just fine without them. If a manufacturer offers several different white varietal glasses, your best bet is to go with their generic, white wine glass, not a "Chardonnay" glass. A basic, "white wine" glass might be referred to as another white wine varietal such as a "Riesling" or a "Viognier" glass, but specifically designated "Chardonnay" glasses are shaped differently than other white varietal glasses.

For a red wine glass choose either a Bordeaux style—also known as Cabernet or Merlot—which is a tall rod-shaped glass, or a Burgundy style—also known as Pinot Noir—which is a large bowl-shaped glass. Pick the style based on what type of reds you are more likely to drink— Cabernets/Merlots or Pinot Noirs. If you really get into certain types of red wines then, by all means, buy the type of glass that best goes with that wine.

For champagne glasses, forget granny's wide-mouthed bubbly bowls and go with flutes instead. Flutes—those long, narrow cylinders— better capture the bubbles. The narrowness of the glass concentrates the fizziness. Plus, they just look more elegant.

Wine Nerd

Have you ever wondered why some champagne flutes create one beautiful string of bubbles from the bottom? Here is the secret, restaurants and glassware manufacturers etch a tiny "x" in the bottom of the glass, giving the bubbles a place to form. You can do the same thing to your flutes using a needle—just be sure to wash the glass thoroughly afterward.

For dessert wine, choose a stout, flute-shaped glass. Dessert wines and ports have a concentrated sweetness and are meant to be drunk in smaller amounts. The smaller glass concentrates the sweeter wine's more intense aromas and tastes.

The number of glasses you get depends on your style of entertaining and budget, but you'll probably want at least four of each type of glass. Decent wine glasses range from $10 to $250 per glass. The price depends on what it is made with and how it is made.

The Benefits of Crystal

For the best effect, choose leaded or optical crystal glasses, preferably hand-blown rather than machine molded.

Crystal has been valued for centuries because its light nature allows the colors of the wine to shine through, and its thin structure allows the wine aromas to be released more fully. In other words, crystal makes the wine taste better. Crystal glasses also have thinner lips around the edge of the glass, which makes for a superior drinking experience.

But the same characteristics that make crystal so appealing also make it delicate. Sometimes, it seems you only have to look at a glass wrong, and it shatters to pieces. Leaded crystal is particularly delicate—and the more expensive the glass, the more likely it is to break. If you tend to break wine glasses frequently, optical crystal glasses are a good alternative to leaded crystal.

Optical crystal is the same stuff used in expensive telescopes, and glassware manufacturer, Bottega del Vino, makes wine glasses with it. Although optical crystal glasses are not indestructible they are a bit stronger than most other crystal glasses, and they can withstand more use and abuse.

Corked

The main problem with stemless glasses is that, just by holding the glass, your hands warm up the wine. That can have an adverse effect on the wine, especially chilled, summer whites.

Whatever type of crystal you purchase, we recommend you stay away from stemless glasses. They were created solely for the purpose of conveniently washing them in dishwashers. Unless you hate handwashing or someone you care about has a dexterity issue—in which case, they're marvelous—stick with stems.

Cleaning Your Wine Glasses

To clean your glasses, use very hot water without dish detergent. If you must use dish detergent, make sure you thoroughly rinse the glasses.

Perfect Pairings

If you don't have tea towels or cheesecloth, paper towels work just fine.

There's nothing worse than drinking a great glass of wine that has a lingering aftertaste of soap. Either air dry the clean glasses upside down on a clean towel or dry them with tea towels. Avoid using towels with lint, as the lint will stick to the glass.

To Decant or Not Decant?

To decant or not decant, that is the question oenophiles sometimes face when planning to uncork an aged, fine vintage. Some people think that they need to decant every fine red wine to fully appreciate it. We recommend decanting only when a red wine has *sediment* at the bottom of the bottle.

Though there is nothing inherently wrong with sediment, it tastes bitter, and nobody likes having to chew their wine. It's kind of like eating a fresh, delicious oyster, and then getting a piece of shell stuck in your teeth. The best way to deal with sediment is to decant it out.

To properly decant a wine, slowly pour the wine out of the bottle and into a separate vessel in one

def•i•ni•tion

Sediment is caused by the breakdown of pigments and tannins within the wine. This bitter-tasting residue usually indicates that the wine is older and that the wine was made with some care. It also typically means that the wine experienced little or no filtration during the wine-making process.

steady stream. Take care not to rock the bottle back while pouring; otherwise, the sediment will move into the new vessel. Although it's more elegant to decant into a crystal wine decanter, you can just as easily decant your wine into a juice carafe or even a clean bottle. You can also filter the wine using a strainer or a coffee filter.

Another reason people decant wine is to open up the wine or to expose wine to air. You might want to do this to a wine that is particularly strong or young to let the wine breathe, so to speak. A strong or young wine might have very sharp, one-dimensional aromas, and decanting will soften them. But generally, we believe decanting is an unnecessary step for enjoying most wines. Some oenophiles obsess about the process of exposing a wine to air so that the aromas are released, but we believe that sometimes decanting releases the aromas prematurely so that you don't get to fully enjoy the wine's complexities as you drink it.

Instead of using a decanter, some people use a more portable device called a "wine aerator." Basically, a wine aerator looks like a small funnel, and the idea is that the wine, being poured first through this contraption, is exposed to air as it is being poured into the glass.

Corked

Some people swear by wine aerators to open up a wine and enhance its flavors. In our opinion, they are useless gadgets, and we don't believe that they make a significant difference.

A Word About Wine Gadgets

It seems as though every year a new wine gadget shows up on the market. Many of them are a waste of money, some are actually pretty useful, and others are downright essential.

The most important wine tool you will need is a good corkscrew. A basic waiter's corkscrew, which costs about $10 to $15, is really all you'll need. Fancier corkscrews abound, but unless you really have problems uncorking wine, this basic model will do the trick.

There are a number of tools available for preserving an open bottle of wine for later use. One is the wine pump. In theory, it pumps the oxygen out of the bottle, thus preserving your wine longer. However, these pumps fail to live up to their promise. But all is not lost; for those times when you don't polish off your bottle, we recommend what many restaurants use to preserve their unfinished bottles, Private Preserve.

Private Preserve is a bottle of air mixed with gases that, when added to the unfinished bottle of wine, pushes the oxygen out of the bottle, protecting the wine. The gases are heavier than the oxygen and create a blanket over the wine, ensuring that the wine doesn't get oxidized. This does not mean you can recork your wine and continue to age it; it simply preserves the wine for anywhere from 5 days to 2 weeks, max. The preserved bottles, unless white or dessert wines, do not have to be refrigerated.

Wine Nerd
Before putting any unfinished bottles of wine in the refrigerator or on the shelf, write the date you opened the bottle on the bottle with a permanent marker so that you know how long it has been open.

For red wine spills on clothes, carpeting, or furniture, Wine Away and other wine stain removers work quite well, but you can also use Jaclyn's special recipe:

Add 2 drops of bleach to 1 cup of seltzer water. Rub with solution until stain is removed then rinse with cool water. *Caution:* Do not use this on dark clothing or carpeting.

Serving Temperatures

Many a good wine has been ruined by serving it at the wrong temperature.

Generally, white, dessert, and sparkling wines should be served chilled, and red wine should be served at what's usually referred to as room temperature. However, in this case "room temperature" actually means cellar or basement temperature, which translates to slightly chilled. If you store your red wines in a cellar, basement, or wine refrigerator, they will already be sufficiently chilled.

For most white, dessert, and sparkling wines, serve them at about 40 to 45 degrees Fahrenheit. In general, rosé wines follow white wine rules.

For most red wines, serve them at about 55 to 60 degrees. Some more complex, aged, white wines should be served at 50 degrees Fahrenheit. An exception to the red wine rule is sweet red wines, like Lambrusco. Treat them as you would white wines.

There's no need to stick a thermometer in your wine to determine its temperature. The following guidelines should do the trick if your wines aren't already stored at the proper temperature:

◆ Chill white wines for about four hours before serving. If you are running late and forgot to chill it, stick it in the freezer for about 20 minutes or put it in an ice bucket with ice, kosher salt, and water.

Corked

More wines are ruined by being served too warm than too cold. Your wine will always warm up in the glass. Err on the chilly side.

♦ Chill red wines for 30 to 60 minutes before serving or stick them in the freezer for about 10 minutes.

Temperature is important not only to the enjoyment of wines, but it also comes into play when pairing wine with foods. Chilled foods— sushi, salads, desserts—are generally paired with chilled wines. Warm, steamy bowls of soup or stew should be paired with warmer, red wines. Too much contrast in temperature could cause a pairing clash that has nothing to do with flavor.

The Least You Need to Know

♦ You only need four types of wine glasses—white, red, champagne, and dessert.

♦ Choose blown crystal stemware as opposed to molded glassware.

♦ Decanting is only necessary when there is sediment in the wine.

♦ White, dessert, and sparkling wines should be served chilled (40 to 45 degrees) while red wines should be served at cellar or basement temperature (55 to 60 degrees).

Part 2

Breaking It Down: Pairing Basics

This part gets to the nitty-gritty of pairings: breaking down wine and food into their basic aromas and flavor profiles for pairing. You'll learn the aromas and flavor profiles of white wines, red wines, sparkling, and dessert wines and how they match with many foods and sauces. You'll also learn about wine characteristics such as weight, alcohol content, sweetness, acidity, and tannins and how they affect the pairing process. We break down each of the major wine varietals for you, providing you with an easy-to-understand explanation of why certain types of wine go best with certain dishes.

4

White Wine's Flavor Profiles

In This Chapter

- ◆ Body and alcohol
- ◆ Sweetness
- ◆ Acidity
- ◆ Rosé's flavor profile
- ◆ Pairing properties of white wines

To properly pair a white wine, you need to be able to discern its various properties, and then understand how those properties mesh with various types of food.

A white wine's body and alcohol content, its residual sugar level, and its acidity all have an impact on how it pairs with food. You'll learn about each of these characteristics, and how they interact with food, in the following pages.

At the end of the chapter, you'll find a list of each major white wine varietal's basic aromas, bouquets, and other properties so you can better pair them with food.

How Body and Alcohol Affect Pairings

Just as milk has a wide range of body, or mouthfeel—from nonfat or skim milk's light body to heavy cream's voluptuous thickness—so does wine. A light wine, like Pinot Gris, has a body similar to that of nonfat milk, whereas a heavy wine, like an aged Chardonnay, has a more substantial body akin to heavy cream or half-and-half.

Typically, the lighter the body, the less alcohol the wine contains. White wines, in general, have lighter bodies and lower alcohol contents than red wines.

When you are pairing white wines with food, you should either match or contrast the weight of the wine with the "weight" of the food. Whether you match or contrast depends on your goal for the pairing. Consider a meal of broiled lobster. Often, when people eat lobster, they're celebrating something and feeling indulgent. If the goal is to enhance this overall feeling of luxury and decadence, then the natural pairing is a creamy, heavy Chardonnay to match the richness of the dish.

But, if you already think that lobster is rich enough on its own, your pairing goal might be to cut down on some of that overindulgence. So instead of a buttery Chardonnay, you might go with a lighter Pinot Gris, or maybe a crisp Spanish Albariño, using the lighter bodied wine to balance out the lobster's decadence.

How Sweet It Is

Many of us began our love affair with wine after sipping a glass of sweet white wine. Perhaps it was a Riesling, maybe even a White Zinfandel, but whatever it was we couldn't get enough of it. Then, over time, our palate evolved, and we acquired a taste for drier wines, leaving all of those sweet wines behind, like a string of discarded lovers.

Unfortunately, that stigma of oversweetened, candylike wines being just for beginners causes many people to overlook off-dry or sweet wines when it comes to pairing wine with anything other than dessert. By doing this, you're writing off a whole world of wonderful pairings and flavor sensations.

Not only that, but sometimes a wine's aromas can trick your taste buds into thinking a wine is sweet when, in reality, it just has a lot of fruity aromas. For this reason, it is common to confuse a "fruity" wine with a truly sweet wine. The reason some wines have a distinctly sweet taste is that they actually contain high amounts of sugar in them. The sugar is leftover from the wine's fermentation process, and it is called residual sugar or R. S. for short.

R. S. is measured in grams per liter or g/L and is sometimes included on a wine's back label. If a bottle indicates that a wine has an R. S. of more than about 15 g/L, the wine will have a slight sensation of sweetness. If the g/L is over 45, be prepared for a lot of sweetness, because that wine is packed with sugar. Dessert wines typically range from 45 g/L to 150 g/L, but can reach as high as 900 g/L!

But not all white wines are sweet, and some wines with a reputation for being sweet, like Riesling, are not always sweet. One thing to note, especially with Rieslings, is that there is a range of sweetness in wines. Some Rieslings are sugary, syrupy, and dripping with sweetness while others are bone-dry. In Germany, there are special terms to help you crack the code of sweetness, but we have an even better key to this code.

> **Perfect Pairings**
>
> Not all Rieslings are sweet. In fact, they can range from bone-dry to sticky-sweet. This makes Rieslings great for a plethora of different pairings. Just be sure to read the label or check with the sommelier to find out how sweet any particular Riesling is.

Another way to estimate the sweetness of the wine is to check its alcohol content, which is listed in small print on the back label. Typically, the less alcohol there is, the more sugar there will be. This means some sugar was not converted into alcohol during the wine-making process. A wine with an alcohol content of 10 percent or more will be drier, whereas a wine with an alcohol content of 4 to 9 percent will be sweeter. But if all else fails and you are not sure, ask the sommelier or the wine shop owner.

While sweet wines sometimes seem to be "heavier" on the tongue, they usually contain less alcohol than drier wines. Their syruplike viscosity can often be an important tool when pairing them with foods.

Sweetness is a good quality to have when pairing foods that are spicy or hot, as the sweetness tends to take the edge off of the spice. Sweeter Rieslings, Gewürztraminers, and Chenin Blancs are sensational alongside curries, stir-fries, and other Asian cuisines not normally associated with wine.

We also love sweeter or off-dry white wines with really salty foods. There is something about these two contrasting flavors that can create a perfect harmony. That something is due to the layout of taste buds on the tongue. Even though the tongue is divided into four different flavor quadrants, sweet and salty overlap each other at the tip of the tongue. So when you take a bite of a kettle-cooked potato chip and follow it with a glass of German Spätlese (sweet) Riesling, the tip of your tongue's flavor receptors will be busy interpreting all that sweet-salty deliciousness.

An Acid Trip

After sweetness, acidity is the most prominent factor taken into consideration when deciding what food to pair with white wines. It is the acidity in white wines that helps them age well, and it is what gives white wines their uplifting, refreshing quality. Crisp, or highly acidic, wines, are delicious with fish, fats, and salads. Just like an acidic green apple, lemon, or lime, such wines uplift the palate.

Acidity has the power to cut through fat and balance out a rich, fatty dish. It can also provide an uplifting quality that helps a wine pair with a refreshing dish like a salad. But if the dish you are pairing with is delicate, or somewhat sweet, you will want to choose a wine with less acidity. Too much acidity can overturn a dish's balance and cause sweeter proteins and foods to taste bitter.

White wines that have a lot of acidity work best when paired with dishes that benefit from the addition of citrus. Take a New Zealand Sauvignon Blanc, for example; the acidity and aroma of this wine is often likened to that of a grapefruit. If you think your dish would be unbalanced with this tangy addition, chances are you don't want to enjoy it with a Sauvignon Blanc. If the dish is something like pan-seared mahi-mahi or a mixed green salad, both of which would welcome the addition of grapefruit, then you have found the right pairing.

Now we can't talk about acidity without mentioning *malolactic fermentation*. This is a secondary fermentation that converts tart, malic acid into the creamy and subtle lactic acid. "M. L.," as oenophiles call it, is what gives many Chardonnays that creamy, rich mouthfeel. Only a small percentage of white wines go through this fermentation, and when they do, they are better suited for pairing with richer foods. It's important to note that while a lot of Chardonnays, especially California Chardonnays, go through M. L., not every Chardonnay experiences this fermentation, so check your bottle or ask the sommelier.

def•i•ni•tion

Malolactic fermentation (M. L.) is a secondary fermentation in which special bacteria convert tart malic acid into softer lactic acid. All red wines go through M. L., but only some white wines do.

Rosy-Cheeked Wines

Rosés—they're not red, they're not white. So what are they? Rosés can be created by one of two processes. Fine rosés are made from the same grapes as red wines, but the skins are removed earlier in the process. Since the grape skins give wine its color, the early removal of the skins imparts a lighter hue. These carefully made pink wines are dry, delicious, and a sommelier's dream.

The second method also uses red grapes and removes their skin earlier than usual, but the wines are then sweetened with reserve grape juice. Wines made in this fashion are typically called blush wines, and are the oversweetened products of the wine boom in California during the 1970s—most notably, White Zinfandel. Wineries like Beringer, Sutter Home, and Mill Creek created these wines in an effort to keep up with the growing demand for white wine. These wines give high-quality rosés a bad reputation.

Corked

Anytime you have a red varietal with the word "white" in front of it, like "White Merlot," you have a sweet, blush wine. These are not traditional rosés.

Good rosés are a nice compromise between white and red wines in pairing situations, making them a great tool for sommeliers. If someone only likes red wine, but the dish would work best with a white wine, have them try a rosé. Do the same if someone prefers white wine with a dish that works best with a red wine.

When pairing rosés, treat them more like white wines than red wines. This is because their body, alcohol, sweetness, and acidity are more like that of a white wine. Also, like white wines, they should be served chilled. Not only can rosés offer an alternative to the white versus red pairings, they also work well with "pink" foods. Salmon, pork, snapper, and tuna all taste divine with a glass of rosé wine.

Let's Get Pairing

Now that you understand how body, alcohol, sweetness, and acidity work, let's take a closer look at these characteristics with specific white wine varietals. There are always exceptions to every varietal, but Jaclyn's master list will help give you the tools to better estimate how a wine will interact with food. Use this list as a basic reference tool when shopping for wine, but also be sure to supplement it with the advice of your friendly wine shop owner or sommelier.

Riesling

Best from   Germany; Alsace, France; Washington; New York; Australia

Body   Light

Alcohol   Low

 Perfect Pairings

Riesling does not pair well with butter. Otherwise it's one of the most versatile wines for pairing.

Acidity   Medium-high

Sweetness   Ranges from very sweet to bone-dry

Common aromas   Lemon, apricot, lime, beeswax, petrol (gasoline), minerals

Best paired with For sweeter Rieslings: soft and blue cheeses; desserts; creole, Thai, curry, and other spicy foods. In general: salty dishes, cheeses, ham, duck, seafood, fruit, salads.

Chenin Blanc

Best from Loire Valley, France; California; South Africa; Australia

Body Light-medium

Alcohol Light-medium

Acidity Medium-high

Sweetness Ranges from sweet to bone-dry

Common aromas Melon, lemon, golden apple, peach

Best paired with Goat cheese; fried foods; mild Chinese, Japanese, and Vietnamese dishes; salads; lighter seafood

Fun fact Also known as "Steen" in South Africa. Can be made into delicious sparkling wines.

Pinot Gris/Grigio

Best from Italy; Alsace, France; Oregon

Body Light-medium

Alcohol Light-medium

Acidity Medium-high

Sweetness Low-medium

Common aromas Lemon, lime, green apple, pear, honeysuckle

Best paired with Raw milk, nutty, and smoked cheeses; cured meats; crudités; seafood, especially shellfish; poultry; lighter pastas

Fun fact Called "Gris" or "Grigio" depending on where it is grown or what style it is molded after. Gris = French (minerally), Grigio = Italy (fruity).

Gewürztraminer

Best from Alsace, France; Alto Adige, Italy; Washington; New Zealand

Body Light-medium

Alcohol Light-medium

Acidity Medium

Sweetness Ranges from sweet to dry

Common aromas Lychee, rose petals, lime curd, passion fruit

Best paired with Semi-soft, smoked, and stinky cheeses; spicy Indian and Asian foods; pork, especially roasted ham; smoked fish and poultry; turkey; tropical fruits

Fun fact Called "Gewürz" for short. Sounds German, but it didn't originate in Germany and is not widely grown there.

Viognier

Best from Rhone Valley, France; California; Australia

Body Medium

Alcohol High-medium

Acidity Low-medium

Sweetness Dry, but can be made semisweet to help balance the high alcohol content.

Common aromas Perfume/flowers, peach, pear, mango, cream

Best paired with Creamy cheeses; cream sauces; spiced dishes especially cinnamon, cumin, and nutmeg; fish

Fun fact Can sometimes be blended with Syrah/Shiraz to offer increased aromatics and finesse.

Grüner Veltliner

Best from   Austria

Body   Medium

Alcohol   Medium-high

Acidity   Medium-high

Sweetness   Dry

Common aromas   Lychee, lime, white pepper, lemon, green beans

Best paired with   Stinky and earthy cheeses; vegetables, especially asparagus; sushi with wasabi

Fun fact   Many people like to claim that no wine pairs well with asparagus and artichokes; however Grüner Veltliner does, making it one of the most versatile wines in the world.

Albariño

Best from   Spain, Portugal, California

Body   Medium

Alcohol   Medium

Acidity   High

Sweetness   Dry

Common aromas   Green apple, peach, almond, salty sea air

Best paired with   Sheep and goat cheeses, seafood, paella, bacon

Fun fact   Also known as Alvarinho in Portugal and used in Vinho Verde white wine blends.

Sauvignon Blanc

Best from   Loire Valley, France; New Zealand; California

Body   Light-medium

Alcohol   Medium

Acidity High

Sweetness Dry

Common aromas Grapefruit, grass, gooseberry, green bell pepper, cat pee (yes, cat pee)

Best paired with Salty and tart cheeses; herbal dishes, especially those with cilantro; raw tomatoes; salads; garlic; vegetables

Fun fact Also known as "Fumé Blanc" in California, partly because of its rich heritage in the village of Pouilly Fumé in France.

> **Corked** _____
>
> Sometimes wines have unusual aromas like cat pee or grass that may seem off-putting. An aroma of cat pee means that a wine has an almost spicy or sharp aroma, but it doesn't mean that the wine tastes as if you're drinking out of the litter box. Wines that have cat pee aromas have a very pleasant acidity that makes them a pleasure to sip.

Pinot Blanc

Best from Alsace, France; California; Oregon

Body Medium-full

Alcohol Medium

Acidity Medium-high

Sweetness Low

Common aromas Apple, melon

Best paired with Mild cheeses; baked vegetables; roasted chicken and turkey; seafood, especially scallops

Fun fact Comes from a genetic mutation of Pinot Noir and Pinot Gris grapes. It is often oaked like Chardonnay since its aromatics are very neutral.

Chardonnay

Best from Burgundy, France; California; South America; Australia; Italy; South Africa

Body   Medium-full

Alcohol   High

Acidity   Medium

Sweetness   Dry

Common aromas   Pineapple, pear, lemon, butter, golden apple, banana, toast, hazelnut

Best paired with   Buttery, creamy cheeses; butter and butter sauces; fried chicken; shellfish, especially crab and lobster; veal; pasta, risotto, and polenta; popcorn

Fun fact   Grown around the world because of its neutral base that showcases its terroir and vinification more than any other white grape. It can range from crisp and minerally (as in Chablis and Champagne, France) to tropical and rich (as in California and Australia).

Dry Rosés

Best from   Anywhere! But traditionally, southern France and Spain.

Body   Light to medium

Alcohol   Medium

Acidity   Medium-high

Sweetness   Dry

Common aromas   Strawberry, raspberry, cranberry, lime peel, rose petals, pepper, mint, flowers

Best paired with   Mild cheeses; charcuterie, especially Serrano ham, pâtés, and smoke-cured poultry; crab and shrimp; summer foods including salads, hot dogs, ribs, sandwiches, and grilled fish—the sky's the limit!

Fun fact   Can be made from any red grape including Syrah, Malbec, Grenache, Cabernet Sauvignon, and Tempranillo. There are even dry Zinfandel rosés from California that are quite good!

The Least You Need to Know

◆ Body, alcohol, and sweetness all affect a white wine's pairing abilities.

◆ Typically, the lighter the wine, the less alcohol it will contain. The lower the alcohol, the sweeter the wine.

◆ Acidity is an important quality to consider when pairing white wines. It can cut through rich dishes, but it can overpower delicate foods. Acidity in wine loves acidity in foods.

◆ Rosés can be considered a bridge between white and red wines; and most of them are not sweet.

◆ Once you understand the basic characteristics of white wines, you'll be able to pair them with food.

Chapter 5

Red Wine's Flavor Profiles

In This Chapter

- Body and alcohol
- Tannins
- The importance of aging
- The odd, sweet red
- Pairing properties of red wines

To properly pair a red wine, you need to first understand how its body and alcohol content affect the wine and how that, in turn, affects the pairing. And don't forget about tannins—those crazy, chemical compounds found in grape skins have a huge impact on how red wines interact with food.

Though some white wines are ageable, typically it is reds that are praised for their long-term ageability. The age of a red wine not only affects its complexity and taste, but its pairing options as well. And while most red wines aren't sweet at all, there are a few sweet reds, adding an interesting twist to the pairing equation.

As we did with white wines in Chapter 4, at the end of the chapter you'll find a list of red wine varietals' characteristics to aid in your pairing endeavors.

How Body and Alcohol Affect Pairings

Many white wines have lithesome, skinny, little bodies that refresh the palate, while many red wines have sexy, voluptuous bodies that fill up your mouth. Although you will encounter white wines that have the body of nonfat milk, you really won't find red wines that have such light mouthfeels. Instead, most red wines have at least a lowfat milklike body, and many of them weigh in on the heavy cream side.

It follows that if red wines have heavier, richer bodies, they should also contain more alcohol than white wines. And, they do. Red wines, on average, contain 11 to 15 percent alcohol, compared to the typical white wine, which contains 9 to 12 percent alcohol. This means that red wines are usually more intense, and they don't typically pair well with delicate foods. That's why, traditionally, red wines have been matched up with heavier, meatier dishes.

It's not that you can't pair red wines with fish or chicken, because you can, but those pairings just aren't as obvious.

All About Tannins

Tannins are chemical compounds found in wines that are derived from the grape's skins, seeds, and stalks. They add to the complexity of red wines and aid in the aging process. As red wines age, tannins break down and smooth out to create a more complex, layered effect in the wines.

Tannins are also found in coffee, tea, and chocolate. They are the substance in red wine that gives it a slightly bitter tang, a textural quality. To better understand and identify what they are, take a plain, red grape and peel the skin back. Now, bite into the skin. Taste that bitter, chalky sharpness? That's the tannin.

> ## Corked
>
> Some people believe they are allergic to red wine because of the tannins. If you aren't allergic to grapes, chances are you aren't allergic to tannins. But you might have another food sensitivity or react negatively to alcohol or histamines. One recent study suggests that it is the histamines in red wine that people are reacting to, rather than the tannins.

Tannins affect pairings in a number of ways. Typically, they add more weight and intensity to a wine, making it necessary to pair it with heavier foods. The more tannic a wine is, the more you will need a strong-flavored food to stand up to it.

Tannins love rich proteins. This is because proteins, like those found in hard cheeses and meat, will give the tannins something to grab on to, causing the wine to taste softer. Tannins also love tannic foods. Some foods like smoked meats, dark chocolate, legumes, and dark berries all have tannins in them; and the tannins in these foods will actually counteract the tannins in a red wine, giving the wine a lighter—even sweet—quality. One of Jaclyn's favorite indulgences is a glass of tannic Zinfandel with a bar of bittersweet chocolate.

When pairing foods with tannic wines, you will also want to be mindful of a dish's salt component. A heavily salted dish can spell disaster when paired with a tannic wine like Syrah. High amounts of salt can cause a wine to taste metallic and overly bitter. For instance, pairing a briny shellfish stew with a tannic Shiraz creates a flavor clash you won't soon forget.

> ## Corked
>
> Salt and tannins react badly with one another. Do not pair a salty dish with a tannic wine.

Aging Gracefully

Many, but not all, red wines can be aged. Some wines, like Beaujolais Nouveau, are meant to be drunk within a year of their release. Other wines, like a mainstream Cabernet Sauvignon, should be consumed within 5 years. But truly great, heavier reds made by exceptional wine-makers, can be aged for 10, 20, even 50 or more years. Whether or not you are that patient is a different story. The truth is, most red wine sold in your local wine shop and grocery store are meant to be consumed young, within 5 years of its vintage. The right time to drink a wine is when you want to drink it, regardless of what any wine snob may say.

If you do choose to age a wine, do so properly. If a bottle of wine has simply been stuck in someone's pantry or at the back of the bar for several years, it may not have been aged at the right temperature or in the right conditions. When aging wine, you want to keep it in a constantly cool, dark place that is free from disturbances and vibrations. You also want to make sure you keep it on its side, not standing straight up. Otherwise when you pop the cork on that "prized" bottle, you could be in for a surprise—in a *bad* way.

> **Perfect Pairings**
>
> If you have a rare, wonderful, aged wine, and you plan to serve it with food, make sure you pair the food to the wine and not the other way around. This is a case where the goal should clearly be to make the food second to the wine.

If you are patient and have properly laid down a bottle of wine in your cellar for a couple decades, chances are you will want to pair it with something that makes the wine the star of the meal. When using aged wines in food pairing, it is important to keep in mind that they are delicate in their old age and should be reserved for foods that will be gentle. So a Cabernet Sauvignon that would have been great with a rib-eye in its youth would be better served with pork or veal in its older age.

Now let's say that you went to the store and picked out a red wine to serve with tonight's dinner, which is more common than grabbing a wine from a personal cellar. If you have selected a lighter, less tannic red it will be best suited for lighter dishes like pork, veal, and even some fish. If you have chosen a red wine that is more complex and heavy, it will work best with heavy, complex dishes like steak au poivre, rack of lamb, or wild boar. When pairing red wine, the bottom line is to match intensity with intensity.

Oddly Sweet

Just as not all Rieslings are sweet, not all reds are dry. In fact, there's a certain subset of red, sweet wines. Now, these wines aren't dripping with sugar like dessert wine, but they do have a bit of sweetness that qualifies them as off-dry. The most likely suspects in this subset are German Spätburgunders, Italian Lambruscos, and even some Australian Shirazes.

Like sweet whites, these reds contain higher amounts of residual sugar. But unlike sweet whites, some of these reds have a bit more alcohol in them. A sweet Shiraz from Australia can contain as much as 15 percent alcohol.

> **Wine Nerd**
>
> Spätburgunder is German for Pinot Noir.

This sweetness needs to be taken into account when pairing. Sweet reds tend to work very well with meats that have a bit more sweetness, like pork. However, they tend to clash with desserts unless the dessert is more on the savory side like a cheesecake made with chèvre (goat cheese) or a blue-cheese tart.

Time to Get Pairing

Now that you understand how body, alcohol, tannins, and—very occasionally—sweetness, affect red wine, let's take a closer look at these characteristics within individual red wine varietals. Once you know a wine's most likely characteristics, you'll be able to pair it better with food. Though there are always exceptions to every varietal, the following master list will help you understand how to pair red wines.

Pinot Noir

Best from Burgundy, France; Oregon; California; New Zealand

Body Light

Alcohol Low-medium

Acidity   Medium-high

Tannin   Low

Sweetness   Can range from off-dry to dry

Common aromas   Ripe cherry, barnyard, raspberry, strawberry

Best paired with   Soft and semi-soft cheeses, roasted chicken, salmon and seared tuna, mushrooms, roasted duck, lamb, pork, veal

Fun fact   Also known as "Pinot Nero" in Italy and Spätburgunder in Germany. In South Africa, it was crossed with another red varietal to create the unique varietal Pinotage, which is very different from Pinot Noir.

Sangiovese

Best from   Tuscany, Italy

Body   Medium

Alcohol   Medium

Acidity   Medium-high

Tannin   Low-medium

Sweetness   Dry

Common aromas   Cherry, tomato, plum, herbs

Best paired with   All sorts of cheese, especially Parmesan, fontina, and taleggio; Italian foods, especially those with tomato; grilled steak or pork

Fun fact   Sangiovese is best known as the main grape utilized in Chianti, but some California producers have planted it to create some delicious "Cal-Ital" wines.

Tempranillo

Best from   Spain

Body   Medium-full

Alcohol   Medium

Acidity   Medium

Tannin   Medium-high

Sweetness   Dry

Common aromas   Cherry, blackberry, plum, tobacco, leather

Best paired with   Hard cheeses, game and game birds, lamb, cured meats

Fun fact   Until just recently, Tempranillo wasn't planted much outside of Spain and Portugal. Australia, Chile, and Argentina are now experimenting with it in blends.

Grenache

Best from   Rhone Valley, France; Spain

Body   Full

Alcohol   High

Acidity   Low

Tannin   Low-medium

Sweetness   Off-dry to dry

Common aromas   Dried cherry, blackberry, currant, earth

Best paired with   Hard cheeses, barbequed and roasted meats, spicy Asian dishes

Fun fact   Called "Garnacha" in Spain. It is usually used in blends because of its lack of color, acidity, and tannins.

Cabernet Sauvignon

Best from   Bordeaux, France; California; South America; Australia; Italy

Body   Full

Alcohol   Medium-high

Acidity   Low-medium

Tannin High

Sweetness Dry

Common aromas Blackcurrant, black cherry, green bell pepper, tobacco, leather

Best paired with Aged, stinky, and blue cheeses; lamb; beef, especially steaks and hamburgers.

Fun fact Cabernet Sauvignon is actually a cross between Cabernet Franc and Sauvignon Blanc, but has a unique character all its own.

Cabernet Franc

Best from Loire Valley and Bordeaux, France; California; Washington

Body Medium-high

Alcohol Medium-high

Acidity Medium

Tannin Medium

Sweetness Dry

Common aromas Violets, dark cherry, plum, green bell pepper

Best paired with Goat and stinky cheeses; eggplant; roasted pork, beef, and lamb; roasted vegetables

Fun fact Cabernet Franc's aromas range from delicate and fruity to herbaceous and peppery. It is one of the few red varietals that is sometimes made into a delicious ice wine.

Merlot

Best from Bordeaux, France; California; Washington; Italy; South America

Body Medium

Alcohol Medium-high

Acidity Medium

Tannin   Medium-high

Sweetness   Dry

Common aromas   Black cherry, plum, green bell pepper

Best paired with   Blue and cheddar cheeses, pizza, roasted beef and pork, roasted and smoked turkey, stews

Fun fact   Miles, a lead character in the movie *Sideways*, slams Merlot, leading a lot of people to swear off this varietal. Ironically, Miles's most treasured wine, Chateau Cheval Blanc, is a blend of Merlot and another varietal he slams, Cabernet Franc. So give Merlot another chance.

Malbec

Best from   Bordeaux and Cahors, France; South America

Body   Medium-full

Alcohol   Medium-high

Acidity   Medium

Tannin   Medium-high

Sweetness   Dry

Common aromas   Plum, dried cherry, blackberry, tobacco

Best paired with   Blue and aged cheeses, grilled beef, bacon, grilled sausages, stews

Fun fact   Malbec has become the national varietal in Argentina largely due to how perfect it pairs with Argentinian cuisine.

Syrah/Shiraz

Best from   Rhone Valley, France; Australia; California

Body   Full

Alcohol   High

Acidity   Medium

Tannin   Medium-high

Sweetness   Can be off-dry, but typically dry

Common aromas   Blackberry, dark cherry, jam, herbs

Best paired with   Aged and hard cheeses; barbeque, especially beef ribs; mushrooms; venison; grilled sausages; wild boar; bittersweet chocolate

Fun fact   In Australia, it is known as "Shiraz" and typically associated with a more intense, concentrated style.

Petite Sirah

Best from   California, Washington, Australia

Body   Full

Alcohol   Medium-high

Acidity   Medium-high

Tannin   High

Sweetness   Dry

Common aromas   Blueberry, blackberry, plum, black pepper, herbs

Best paired with   Aged and hard cheeses, roasted and grilled game, Mexican food

Fun fact   Even though their names are similar names, Petite Sirah and Syrah are completely unrelated.

Zinfandel

Best from   California, Italy

Body   Medium-full

Alcohol   High

Acidity   Medium

Tannin   Medium-high

Sweetness   Dry

Common aromas   Raspberry, blackberry, cherry, pepper, anise

Best paired with   Blue cheeses; meats in sweet barbeque sauces; spicy cuisines like Creole, Mexican, and Thai; pizza; Andouille sausage; roasted turkey

Fun fact   Some still debate it, but Primitivo in Italy and Zinfandel are genetically the same grape.

The Least You Need to Know

- ◆ Red wines tend to have more body and higher alcohol content than white wines.

- ◆ The more tannic a red wine, the heavier the food needs to be for a perfect pairing.

- ◆ Consider the age of a red wine when pairing it with food.

- ◆ Sweet red wines should be paired differently than their dry counterparts.

- ◆ Once you understand the basic characteristics of red wines, you can start pairing them with food.

Chapter 6

Sparkling and Dessert Wines' Flavor Profiles

In This Chapter

- ◆ All about the bubbles in bubbly
- ◆ Types of sparklers
- ◆ Defining sweetness in dessert wines
- ◆ Botrytized, late harvest, and fortified wines
- ◆ Pairing properties of sparkling and dessert wines

All sparkling and dessert wines are not created equal, and this chapter explains their differences and how these variations affect pairings.

To properly pair these wines with food you must first grasp their levels of sweetness, viscosity, and, with sparklers, the quality of their bubbles.

Many people enjoy Champagne and sparkling wines on New Year's Eve and other festive occasions, but these effervescent beauties shouldn't just be reserved for special celebrations.

They're actually one of the most versatile wine styles for pairing, and they even go with some childhood favorites, including mac 'n cheese and chicken nuggets.

While people often reserve sparklers for special occasions, they tend to avoid dessert wines altogether. Sometimes people shy away from dessert wines just because they are unfamiliar with them. If you've graduated from White Zinfandel to heavier Cabs and Syrahs, dessert wines might seem like taking a step backwards in your taste progression. But dessert wines are nothing like the sweet wines you may have enjoyed in college. They are a luxurious experience, and there's nothing more sublime than a perfectly paired dessert wine. If you think you love chocolate cake, wait until you try it paired with a Ruby Port or late harvest Zin. Heaven awaits, and this chapter will introduce you to some sweet delights.

Bubble Up

Sparkling wines wear many hats. They can be syrupy sweet, but they can also be bone-dry. They can be white, pink, or red, and they can be made from dozens of different grapes. But what puts sparklers into their very own category is carbonation. When it comes to sparkling wine, the bubbles are what make them special.

Bubbles provide the uplifting quality that many people associate with celebrations. But by limiting the drinking of these wines to just special occasions, you are missing out on a plethora of pairing possibilities. Bubbles are exceptionally good at cutting through creaminess and offering your palate a fresh start.

But not all bubbles are created equal. The size of the bubbles is very important. The smaller the bubble, the finer the wine; likewise, the bigger the bubble, the lesser the wine.

Wine Nerd
Not all sparkling wines are Champagnes. Champagne is a region in France that is known for making some of the best sparkling wines in the world, and only sparkling wines that come from that region are called Champagnes. All other bubblies are referred to as sparkling wines.

In most cases, fine, small bubbles are created through the traditional method of making Champagne or sparkling wine, also known as *méthode traditionelle* or *méthode champenoise*. With this technique, the bubbles are created through a special process of fermentation and aging in the bottle. Méthode traditionelle not only creates finer bubbles, but it can also create secondary, "yeasty" aromas that make these wines perfect for pairing with breads and baked items.

def•i•ni•tion

Méthode traditionelle, also known as **méthode champenoise,** is the process of making sparkling wines in which the fermentation takes place within the bottle, producing finer bubbles and thus a higher-quality wine.

The bubbles in less expensive sparkling wines are created through tank fermentation, a process that produces larger bubbles and less complex wines. The bubbles in the cheapest sparklers are made by injecting carbonation into the wine, just like you would make a soda.

What does bubble size have to do with pairing? Balance. Not only are its bubbles more even and uniform, but the wine's flavors and aromas are typically more balanced as well, indicating that the wine has been made with more care. Plus, those tiny little bubbles just feel better on your tongue. So when you have balance and a sensation that tickles your tongue, you are better equipped to make a successful pairing.

The $3 sparklers that go on sale in liquor stores every New Year's Eve are, obviously, not the way to go if you want to pair up a bubbly with food. But you also don't necessarily have to pony up $200 for a bottle of Dom Pérignon. Fine sparkling wines, especially those from Spain and California, can be had for $15 to $40 a bottle.

But the quality of the bubbles isn't the only thing to consider when pairing with sparkling wine. The quantity of bubbles is also important. Many sparkling wines are jam-packed with bubbles, but there also are lightly sparkling wines, too. *Frizzante* and *petulante* are words that describe lightly bubbled wines. Going easier on the bubbles can help when pairing more delicate and highly textural foods such as chalky goat cheese.

From Sweet to Dry: Reading a Sparkling Label

Champagnes and sparkling wines pair well with both sweet and savory dishes. You can pair them with appetizers, entrées, and desserts. But not every Champagne or sparkling wine works with every course.

To figure out which bubbly to serve with your dish, you first need to know its level of sweetness. As a general rule, wines labeled "brut" are dry, and everything else is some degree of sweet.

From sweetest to driest, the sparklers are classified as: doux, demi-sec, sec, extra brut, brut, and brut nature.

When pairing sparklers with desserts, choose doux or demi-sec sparkling wines. For savory dishes, go for the extra brut, brut, or brut nature. You can pair sec sparkling wines with savory dishes that have a sweet component, like apple roasted pork. It can bridge the gap and create a happy medium. The level of sweetness or dryness you choose will be based on your pairing goals as well as the dish itself.

For savory dishes, brut is better with rich and creamy, protein dishes such as scallops; while brut nature brings out the best of brinier and drier dishes like steamed mussels.

> **Corked**
>
> *Doux* means sweet in French, and doux sparklers are, appropriately, the sweetest. Confusingly, however, *sec* means dry in French, yet demi-sec and sec sparklers are not completely dry; instead, they are semi-sweet and off-dry.

> **Perfect Pairings**
>
> Dry sparkling wines pair up very well with fried foods. The bubbles are able to cut through the fat and pair perfectly with the crunchy exterior of the dish, while still being delicate enough for the moist interior of the food.

Grape Expectations

Sparkling wines are made from many different types of grapes. Basically, any wine can be made sparkling as long as it is fermented under pressure. So there are sparkling Rieslings, Chenin Blancs, and even Shirazes. But classic Champagne is always made from just three grapes—Chardonnay, Pinot Noir, and Pinot Meunier.

Many other sparkling wines around the world are modeled after Champagnes and process those three grapes in their various *cuvées.* When they use only white grapes in the blend, they are sometimes labeled "blanc de blancs." This style of sparkling wine is typically higher in acidity and lighter in body. If there are only red grapes in the cuvée, it will be labeled as a "blanc de noirs." This style is usually suited for slightly heavier foods, as it often has a heavier body.

def•i•ni•tion

The word **cuvée** simply means "blend" in French and refers to the specific blend of varietals used to create a specific sparkling wine.

Knowing the grapes is important in pairing because, although the wines are all sparkling, the aromas and characteristics of the individual grapes will shine through in the final product.

This means that if you know Chardonnay grapes have aromas of pineapple and citrus and have a higher acidity, and Pinot Noir has berry aromas and a fuller-body, then the resulting sparkling wine will likely have a complex aroma, body, and structure of the two grapes combined. Once you understand the aromas and characteristics of a grape (see Chapters 4 and 5), you'll be able to match the wine to the flavors of a dish.

Though most sparklers are clear or white in color, there are rosé and red sparkling wines, too. Rosé sparkling wines are made in the same way rosé wines are created, and red sparkling wines are made in the same way red wines are created. The difference between the sparklers and their still counterparts is that they undergo fermentation under pressure to create those bubbles.

Red sparkling wines are primarily made in Australia, Italy, and France (French ones aren't often exported, though). Probably the most well-known red sparkling wine is Italy's sweet Lambrusco. Lambrusco's sweetness, however, is more of an exception, as red sparkling wines tend to be drier and more tannic in nature. Australia's red bubblies are most

---

Wine Nerd

Aussies love their clever wine names. Some of their more playful names for sparkling Shiraz wines are Black Bubbles, Naked on Rollerskates, and Goosebumps.

often made from Shiraz grapes and often have peppery, spicy aromas and heavier tannins. Don't let their effervescence fool you though—they have more weight and structure than any other sparkling wine out there. Their stronger aromas and characteristics make them more suitable with heavier, meatier dishes.

Dessert Wines

Not all dessert wines are created equal. Their varying degrees of sweetness, along with differing degrees of body or viscosity, must be taken into account when pairing.

From the sweet, to very sweet, some of the best dessert wines are Sherry, Madeira, Port, Vin Santo, late harvest wine, ice wine, Moscato, Sauternes, and Tokaji.

Corked

When pairing wines with dessert, always make sure the wine is sweeter than the dessert. Even if the wine tastes sweet on its own, it might not taste sweet when it is paired with an even sweeter dessert.

The main reason to know the level of sweetness is that whenever you pair a dessert wine with an actual dessert, the wine *must* be sweeter than the dessert. Otherwise, the dessert will not only overpower the wine, but it will make the wine taste bitter, or even sour. If you are unsure of the sweetness level of a wine, check the back label for the amount of residual sugar it contains.

Some dessert wines, such as Port, Sherry, and Madeira, are fortified, meaning they are sweetened by adding alcohol during the fermentation process and so they have a bit more alcohol in them than other wines. They often start at 15 percent alcohol content and they go up from there. As such, they typically have a fuller body or weight to them. The residual sugar in these wines also tends to make them quite viscous. Because they are so weighty, fortified wines are best paired with richer, more intensely sweet and robust flavors. A little dessert wine goes a long way: a typical serving size is only a few ounces.

And just because they are called "dessert" wines you don't have to drink them exclusively with sweets. They also pair well with rich foods such as charcuterie and cheeses. A rich, savory helping of *foie gras* is heavenly with a glass of dessert wine. Again, it is that contrasting sweet and salty combination that makes your taste buds sing.

Botrytized and Late Harvest Dessert Wines

Botrytized and late harvest dessert wines are two of the most intense kinds of dessert wines out there. These wines' grapes are harvested late into the season in order to allow them to develop more sugar content and even raisinate (shrivel like raisins) a bit.

Often late harvest wines are labeled with their varietal, like Zinfandel, Riesling, and Syrah. *Ice wines* are made from grapes left on the vine so long that they freeze, causing the grape to lose moisture and intensify the remaining sugar and flavor. *Botrytized* means the grapes have been left on the vine so long that a mold has grown on them.

def•i•ni•tion

> **Ice wine** is also known as "Eiswein" in Germany and Austria. Some of the best ice wines can be found in upstate New York and Canada. They usually come in 375 ml half bottles and can carry a hefty price tag. But keep in mind that a little of these wines goes a long way.
>
> **Botrytized** refers to the process of cultivating grapes so that a special mold or rot called **botrytis cinera** grows on the grapes.

This "noble rot," as it is called, dehydrates the grapes and concentrates their sweetness. The resulting wines have very concentrated, honeylike aromas with a tinge of mineral and metallic aromas, too.

The most famous botrytized wine is one from Sauternes, an area in Bordeaux, France. These rich, syrupy wines are often referred to as "liquid gold" by wine lovers. Sauternes are intense, apricot- and honey-filled dessert wines that are delicious as a contrast to salty foods.

Fortified Wines: Port, Madeira, and Sherry

Fortified wines like Ports, Madeiras, and Sherries all have additional alcohol added to them during their wine-making process. This extra alcohol needs to be taken into account when pairing because the additional alcohol gives these wines more intensity.

> **Perfect Pairings**
>
> Bittersweet chocolates—especially those of 80 percent cacao or more—often pair well with dry reds like Zinfandel and Syrah. When pairing sweeter milk and white chocolates, reach for a bottle of Ruby or White Port.

They typically should not be paired with delicate desserts like meringues or light pastries. Instead look to richer, more robust desserts for pairing possibilities. The nutty aromas of Tawny Ports, Madeiras, and Sherries are great with nutty desserts like pecan pie and almond tortes. Ruby Ports pair very well with chocolate desserts, thanks to their rich fruitiness that interacts well with chocolate.

Sherries tend to fall into one of three categories: dry, medium, and sweet. When pairing with desserts, go for the sweet varieties. Try sweet Sherries, known as "Jerez Dulce" in Spanish. Those that are labeled "Cream" or "PX" are best suited for dessert. Other types of Sherry, like Fino and Manzanilla, can be shockingly dry and are not suited for dessert pairings.

Madeira wines, made on the Portuguese island of Madeira, are created through a process called estufagem, in which the wines are heat-aged after fermentation and fortification.

> **Wine Nerd**
>
> The process of fortification came about as a solution to keeping wine good for long voyages. When ships would sail around the world, their wine would quickly oxidize and go bad. By adding extra alcohol, the wine kept much longer.

Before the advent of gasoline, or even steam engines, Madeira was shipped on long voyages across the Atlantic. As the wine sat out on the deck, it would age and intensify, creating the style of Madeira that we are familiar with. Today, Madeira makers recreate this sealike atmosphere by using heated rooms and sunshine.

Madeiras are typically labeled by the main grape varietal used to make them. Bual and Malvasia are the sweetest. Sercial and Verdelho tend to be more off-dry. There are also generic Madeiras that use a dryness scale, much like sparkling wines, to define their style. Any Madeira labeled "doce" is suitable for dessert pairings, especially desserts made with nuts or coffee.

Pour Some Sugar on Me

Dessert wines are so sweet and filling they can be enjoyed as a dessert in their own right, no food pairing necessary. Because they are so sweet and filled with rich aromas, they also can add an interesting note to the actual desserts themselves. You can pour some Port over a dense, flourless chocolate cake, drizzle some late harvest Riesling over a fruit salad, and even sprinkle some Sherry over vanilla ice cream.

In fact, if you are pressed for time and want to dress up a store-bought dessert, pour a dessert wine over a cheesecake, pound cake, or ice cream, garnish with whipped cream, and you've got a sensational dessert.

Perfect Pairings

If you plan on drinking some dessert wine with your dessert, pair the dessert with whatever wine you poured over it. Not only will the wine enhance the dessert's flavors, but it will match perfectly!

Putting It All Together

Now that you understand the properties and characteristics of both sparkling and dessert wines, let's take a closer look at how these characteristics work within individual wines. Once you know a wine's most likely characteristics, you'll be able to pair it better with food. Though there are always exceptions, Jaclyn's master list of sparkling and dessert wines will help you better understand how to pair them with food.

Cava

Place of origin   Penedès, Spain

Grape(s)   Macabeo, Parellada, Xarel-lo, Trapat for rosés

How it is made   Méthode traditionelle

Common aromas   Citrus, brioche, minerals

Best paired with   Firm and hard cheeses, fried fish, sushi, egg dishes (especially with rosés), tapas

Fun fact   Cava, in general, is one of the best values in sparkling wine. The word "cava" comes from the word "cave" and refers to the caves that the bottles are aged in during secondary fermentation.

Prosecco

Place of origin   Veneto, Italy

Grape(s)   Prosecco

How it is made   Tank method

Common aromas   Yellow apple, peach, pear

Best paired with   Soft and mild cheeses, Chinese food, shrimp, brunch foods

Fun fact   Can be fully sparkling (spumante) or lightly sparkling (frizzante). Great for use in brunch cocktails, such as bellinis and mimosas.

Champagne

Place of origin   Champagne, France

Grape(s)   Chardonnay, Pinot Noir, Pinot Meunier

How it is made   Méthode traditionelle

Common aromas   Apple, pear, pineapple, citrus, brioche, chalk

Best paired with   In general: All types of cheese, caviar, oysters, butter sauces, fried food, popcorn, sushi, and fish. Rosé: Beef carpaccio, lamb, berries, pink fishes, quail. Blanc de Blancs: Seafood, especially sushi. Blanc de Noirs: Smoked seafood and egg dishes. Dry Champagne: Anything but sweet foods.

Fun fact   Champagne can be used for more than just celebrations. It goes great with virtually everything and can be enjoyed as an everyday indulgence with something as simple as fried chicken and french fries.

Sparkling Shiraz

Place of origin   Australia

Grape(s)   Shiraz

How it is made   Carbonation

Common aromas   Blackberry, strawberry, cherry, cocoa, violets, vanilla, beef

Best paired with   Blue cheese, dark chocolate, fresh berries, steak, French toast, waffles with maple syrup

Fun fact   Make sure you chill your sparkling Shiraz before you open it. If it is too warm, it can be quite explosive and create a horrible, staining mess. This is one red wine that should be served ice cold.

Sherry

Place of origin   Jerez, Spain

Grape(s)   Palomino, Moscatel, Pedro Ximenez

How it is made   Fortification. Brandy is added after fermentation. Because of this, most Sherries start out dry and are sweetened with the addition of reserve sweet wine.

Common aromas   Nuts, caramel

Best paired with   Blue cheese, almonds, baked apple desserts, nut based pies and tarts, cream based soups

Fun fact   Look at the bottling date on the back of the bottle. Be sure to buy a bottle that has been labeled no more than a year prior to your purchase date.

Madeira

Place of origin   Madeira Islands, Portugal

Grape(s)   Malvasia, Bual, Verdelho, Sercial

How it is made   Fortification. Fermentation is halted with the addition of brandy. Then the wine is aged in casks in the sun or a saunalike room to concentrate flavors and sweetness.

Common aromas   Raisins, coffee, caramel

Best paired with   Blue or mild cheeses; banana, nut, caramel, and milk chocolate desserts; pumpkin and squash

Fun fact   Madeira was the wine of choice for early Americans; in fact, it was used to toast the signing of the Declaration of Independence. It lasts nearly forever, when properly stored, so go ahead and invest in a good bottle.

Tawny Port

Place of origin   Douro, Portugal

Grape(s)   Tinta Barroca, Tinta Cão, Tinta Roriz (Tempranillo), Touriga Francesa, and Touriga Nacional

How it is made   Fortification. Various vintages are blended together and aged in barrels.

Common aromas   Nuts, vanilla, caramel

Best paired with   Cheddar and hard cheeses, apples, dried fruits, nuts, and dark chocolate

Fun fact   Tawny Ports are usually labeled with the number of years the youngest component of the wine has been aged in oak. So a 10-year-old tawny has all been in oak for at least 10 years.

Ruby Port

Place of origin   Douro, Portugal

Grape(s)   Tinta Barroca, Tinta Cão, Tinta Roriz (Tempranillo), Touriga Francesa, and Touriga Nacional

How it is made   Fortification. The wine is kept bright and fruity by storing the wine in stainless steel or concrete vats instead of barrels prior to bottling.

Common aromas   Cherry, blackberry, plum, raisins

Best paired with   Blue cheese; dark chocolate desserts, especially cake; berry pies

Fun fact   Ruby Port is the most inexpensive Port-style wine and typically does not improve with age. Some Australian and Californian wineries have created their own ruby styled Ports that are quite good and a great value, too.

Late Harvest Reds

Place of origin   Worldwide

Grape(s)   Endless possibilities. Most commonly: Syrah, Zinfandel, Petite Sirah, and Cabernet Franc.

How it is made   Late harvest. Grapes are left on the vines to raisinate and intensify, then they are partially fermented to retain some sugar.

Common aromas   Dark cherry, bramble fruit, plum, raisin, chocolate

Best paired with   Blue cheese, fruit desserts, chocolate

Fun fact   Any red grapes can be made into late harvest wine as long as they don't rot before they are harvested.

Vin Santo

Place of origin   Tuscany, Italy

Grape(s)   Trebbiano, Malvasia, Canaiolo

How it is made   Passito method. The grapes are picked and dried out on straw mats or by being hung from rafters. The resulting raisins are then pressed and fermented.

Common aromas   Dried cherry, dried peach, nuts, honey

Best paired with   Biscotti, hazelnut desserts, pastries, cakes (any flavor except chocolate)

Fun fact   This wine is believed to have originated as a wine used during Catholic Mass, but today it is made for global consumption.

Late Harvest Whites/Ice Wines

Place of origin   Cool regions, worldwide

Grape(s)   Endless possibilities. Most commonly: Riesling, Gewürztraminer, and Seyval Blanc.

How it is made   Late harvest. Grapes are left on the vines to raisinate and intensify. With ice wine they are allowed to freeze on the vine. Then they are partially fermented to retain some sugar.

Common aromas   Honey, apricots, peach, pear, dried apples, lychee

Best paired with   Soft or blue cheeses, shortbread, creamy desserts (like panna cotta or cheesecake), fruit desserts

Fun fact   Ice wines are often quite expensive because leaving grapes on the vine to freeze is a very risky process and often produces very low yields.

Sauternes

Place of origin   Bordeaux, France

Grape(s)   Sauvignon Blanc, Semillon, Muscadelle

How it is made   Botrytis. The grapes are left on the vine to develop the "noble rot" then handpicked and slow fermented.

Common aromas   Honey, dried apricot, minerals

Best paired with   Blue cheese; foie gras; peach, pear, apple, and other fruit desserts; crème brûlée

Fun fact   Chateau d'Yquem is the most famous and expensive of all Sauternes. They send their grape pickers out into the vineyard several times a day to pick only grapes that are at optimal ripeness.

Tokaji

Place of origin   Hungary

Grape(s)   Furmint, Hárslevelü

How it is made   Botrytis. Affected grapes are picked and then made into a paste. Must is added to the paste and the resulting juice is slowly fermented and then put into casks to age.

Common aromas   Honey, apricot, orange peel, quince

Best paired with   Blue and creamy cheeses, custard, pastries, fruit-based desserts

Fun fact   Tokaji Aszú wines are ranked by sweetness using a "puttony number." Three puttonyos is lightly sweet and moderately intense, while 6 puttonyos is very sweet and intense. Anything over 6 puttonyos is called Aszú-Eszencia and is highly concentrated, quite sweet, and very rare.

The Least You Need to Know

- Not all bubbles are created equal; the smaller the bubble, the better the wine.

- From sweet to dry, sparkling wines are classified as doux, demi-sec, sec, extra brut, brut, and brut nature.

- Pair desserts with doux, demi-sec, or sec sparklers; pair savory dishes with extra brut, brut, or brut nature sparklers.

- Always make sure the dessert wine is sweeter than the actual dessert.

- Botrytized and late harvest grapes create extremely sweet wines.

- Fortified wines have extra alcohol added to them, and that needs to be taken into account when pairing.

7

The Flavor Profiles of Food

In This Chapter

- How cooking changes food's flavor profiles
- How rubs, sauces, and seasonings affect pairings
- Picking out a dish's predominant flavors
- Common ingredients and their pairings

Even though we all know how food tastes, there's more to flavor than meets the tongue. When it comes to pairing food with wine, in addition to an ingredient's basic taste, you must also consider how it is cooked, seasoned, and combined with other ingredients. Only after you have taken all of these elements into consideration can you even begin to start thinking about what wine to serve with it.

One of the most challenging aspects of pairing food with wine is picking out the predominant flavors of a dish, and then matching those flavors with a wine that will complement them. In an effort to more easily pair foods with wines, we've come up with a master list of over 100 ingredients and their perfect pairs.

How Cooking Changes Flavors

While some foods, such as crudités and sushi, can be paired raw, most foods we pair are cooked in some manner. Different methods of cooking impart different flavors, resulting in seemingly endless possibilities for pairing.

Cooking changes not only the texture and temperature of foods, but also their taste. Boiling/poaching, roasting/baking/toasting, frying, grilling, and smoking all lead to vastly different flavor components.

Boiling or poaching has an almost neutral effect on a food's taste. It might change the texture, but the overall flavors remain true to the dish's original ingredients. Think of a boiled potato or a piece of poached chicken, these cooking methods only mildly affect the taste. For boiled or poached foods, you will probably need to pay more attention to the seasonings you add to these dishes instead of how the cooking impacts the flavor of the ingredients.

Roasting and baking both impart another layer of flavor and complexity. They enhance or intensify flavors. Think of a baked or roasted potato, the potato's skin gets a little crispier, perhaps a bit caramelized, and the potato itself becomes a little sweeter. For roasting or baking, you will probably want a wine that has been aged in neutral oak to match the intensity of the cooking method.

Toasting or browning foods adds secondary flavors and complexity. You add sweetness, but also a bit of charring. For pairing, you'll want to go with a wine that has been aged in oak.

Grilling adds even more depth and complexity than toasting, calling for a wine with a heavier body and more intense aromas. Pairing grilled foods with a wine that has been aged in new oak or charred oak barrels will mimic the flavor of the grilling, because the oak adds body, weight, and tannins to the wine.

Smoking foods concentrates flavors even more so than grilling. It adds complexity, sweetness, and intensity. Pair smoked foods with a wine that has a heavier body and more tannin to stand up to that smoke flavor. A wine with a smoky aroma, which usually comes from aging in charred oak barrels or its terroir, will also help in these pairings.

Frying not only alters the original food's flavor but also adds fat to the dish; additionally, the oils used to fry the food add even more flavor. Different oils impart different flavors, too. Take french fries: If you cook them in duck fat, you'll want a wine that has more body, such as a lightly oaked Chardonnay; but if you cook them in corn oil, a simple Pinot Gris will do just fine. When pairing with fried foods, you also might want to consider a wine that has enough acidity to cut through that fat or something with bubbles.

> **Perfect Pairings**
>
> Certain terroirs, like South Africa and South America, offer wines that have smokier, more intense aromas. This makes their wines a good fit with more intense, smoky dishes.

How to Examine Basic Ingredients

Most of us know what foods taste like, but that doesn't mean we know how to pair those tastes with wine. Here are some simple things to keep in mind when looking at fruits, vegetables, cheeses/dairy products, seafood/fish, poultry, and meats.

With fruits, keep in mind their degree of sweetness and the amount of acidity. Both sweetness and acidity amounts can change depending on how the fruit is prepared. Think of fresh strawberries versus strawberry jam. The jam contains less acidity, but it is sweeter than the fresh berries. When pairing fruits with wine, you want to match their levels of acidity. With an acidic fruit dish, a wine with only light acidity will get lost and pair up poorly.

With vegetables, consider the starch content and bitterness. Think of jicama versus celery, or arugula versus butter lettuce.

With very starchy vegetables, acidity is important in choosing a wine to pair. Pair starchy veggies with wines that have a crisp acidity to contrast. **With vegetables that have a degree of bitterness,** steer clear of tannic wines. Tannic wines and bitter veggies equal a bad, mouth-puckering experience. In this case, pair opposites. Pair bitter veggies with light wines.

Perfect Pairings

Match a bitter vegetable, like arugula, with a light, crisp wine like Sauvignon Blanc. Not only will its herbaceous aromas play well with the arugula, its acid content will help neutralize the arugula's bitterness. It's a delightful matchup.

Perfect Pairings

If you absolutely must pair a red wine with a more delicate cheese, grate a little fresh pepper on top of the cheese. The pepper will tie the cheese and the wine together, and it will prevent the tannins from clashing with the cheese.

With cheeses and dairy products, consider the intensity. Aged and blue cheeses can stand up to stronger wines, while fresh and mild cheeses will be overwhelmed by heavier wines. Wines with acidity can cut through the fat and richness of both cheeses and cream sauces. Sweeter wines tend to pair better with cheeses in general; and white wines, overall, work better with cheeses than red wines.

Seafood, fish, and poultry all usually offer more neutral flavors and serve more as a canvas for the seasoning or preparation methods. Pair them according to their seasonings or how they were prepared.

Meats contain more fat and more intensity, both of which need to be considered when pairing. Tannic wines tend to pair well with meats, as do more complex wines in general. How the meat was raised can also affect the pairing. Pasture-grazed versus corn-fed makes a difference in the pairing. Pasture grazing results in richer, more intense flavors, which means the wine needs to be richer or more intense.

The quality of the food, whether it is fruit or meat, also plays a role. Higher-quality foods tend to have more intense flavors. This can be particularly true when choosing local produce. A fresh berry, harvested at the peak of summer, offers fresher, sweeter, more intense flavors than one flown in from South America and ripened in a truck. As a result, you will need to pair local foods with more intense wines.

Fine or rare ingredients—whether imported or domestic—can also change a dish. Certain, canned tunas imported from Spain or Italy, for example are a lot more flavorful than the grocery store varieties. You need to be aware of your ingredients' properties when pairing.

Rubbing in Flavor

Rubs and seasonings both change the flavors of food and most definitely affect pairings. Rubs often impart more salt directly to the food, which you should balance with more fruit in the wine. A salt-cured beef tenderloin, for example, needs a rich, fruity red like a Zinfandel rather than an earthy Cabernet Sauvignon.

With seasonings, consider the intensity of the seasonings themselves, as not all spices are created equal. Tahitian vanilla has a fruitier, more complex flavor than plain old vanilla extract. And Spanish paprika is hotter and more intense than Hungarian paprika. With heavily seasoned sauces, determine whether you want to highlight the main dish or the sauce. Is it the beef tenderloin you are pairing to, or is it the peppercorn cream sauce?

> **Perfect Pairings**
>
> Brining does not necessarily alter the food's basic properties. While it enhances the moisture of meats and poultry, it doesn't add more salt to the meat (despite the vast amount of salt used in the brine itself), and as such, it doesn't affect the pairing much.

Making Flavors Sing in Pairings

When you consider a whole dish for pairing, first you need to pick out its predominant flavors. Concentrate on pairing those top two or three tastes with a wine's aromas.

Keep in mind that the predominant flavors of a dish are not always the ingredients that are used in the largest amounts in a recipe. Rosemary and olive oil roasted chicken, for example, typically doesn't use a lot of rosemary, but rosemary is definitely a predominant flavor to consider when pairing that dish.

> **Perfect Pairings**
>
> Rosemary, olive oil, and garlic are three examples of ingredients that, in small amounts, can have a big impact on a dish's final flavors.

And keep in mind that you don't always have to pair with the main entrée. If you've got some great ribeye steaks and you're planning to serve the steaks with roasted potatoes and baked zucchini casserole, you're probably going to choose a wine that pairs with the ribeyes. But if the zucchini casserole is a family favorite and the star of the meal, you might want to concentrate on the casserole instead.

Putting It all Together

Although the ingredients in most foods we eat have been combined and cooked, the basic flavors of the individual ingredients often shine through.

To better understand how ingredients match up with wines, Jaclyn has created a master pairings list for more than 100 common ingredients, including meats, cheeses, vegetables, fruits, seafood, fish, herbs, and spices. When using this list, it is important to consider the intensity of the dish as a whole and pair the wine that matches up with that from among the recommendations.

Almond   *See* Nuts

Anchovy   Dry rosé, dry Sherry, Pinot Grigio

Apple   Riesling, Gewürztraminer, Chenin Blanc

Apricot   Riesling, Chenin Blanc, late harvest white wines

Artichoke   Grüner Veltliner, Blanc de Blancs Champagne, Sauvignon Blanc

Asparagus   Grüner Veltliner, Sauvignon Blanc, unoaked Chardonnay

Avocado   Chardonnay, Sauvignon Blanc, Brut Champagne, Grüner Veltliner

Bacon   Chardonnay, Pinot Noir, Syrah, Tempranillo

Banana   Madeira, Tawny Port, Blanc de Blancs Champagne

Basil   Sangiovese, Sauvignon Blanc, unoaked Chardonnay, Zinfandel

Beans   Shiraz, Zinfandel, Rhone blends

Beef   Cabernet Sauvignon, Syrah/Shiraz, French Pinot Noir

Bell Pepper   Sauvignon Blanc, Viognier, Cabernet Sauvignon, Cabernet Franc

Berries   Sparkling wines, Riesling, Beaujolais, red wines with various berry flavors, Ruby Port

Bread   Chardonnay, sparkling wine

Broccoli   Sauvignon Blanc, Grüner Veltliner

Butter   Chardonnay, sparkling wine

Capers   Sauvignon Blanc, Pinot Gris/Grigio, Pinot Noir

Caramel   Tawny Port, Madeira, sweet Sherry, late harvest white wines

Carrot   Grüner Veltliner, Sémillon, Viognier, Riesling

Cauliflower   Pinot Gris, off-dry Riesling

Cheese, any kind   Riesling

Cheese, bloomy rind   Sparkling wine, Riesling, Beaujolais, Sherry, Gewürztraminer

Cheese, blue   Dessert wines, Ports, Cabernet Sauvignon, Merlot

Cheese, cheddar   Chardonnay, Cabernet Sauvignon, Pinot Noir, Sherry

Cheese, goat   Sauvignon Blanc, Chenin Blanc, Pinot Gris/Grigio

Cheese, hard   Red wine, especially Italian

Cheese, Swiss   Gewürztraminer, Pinot Noir, Grenache

Cheese, washed rind (stinky)   French Pinot Noir, Blanc de Noirs Champagne

Chicken   Chardonnay, Pinot Noir, Riesling

Chickpeas   *See* Hummus

Chiles   Riesling, Chenin Blanc, Sauvignon Blanc, Shiraz

Chocolate, dark   Port, Zinfandel, Shiraz/Syrah, Petite Sirah

Chocolate, milk   Madeira, Tokaji, Sherry, Vin Santo

Chocolate, white   Late harvest whites, Moscato

Cilantro   Riesling, Sauvignon Blanc

Cinnamon   Pinot Noir, Gewürztraminer

Clams   Chardonnay, Pinot Gris/Grigio, Cava, Albariño

Clove   Gewürztraminer, Zinfandel

Coconut   Oaked Chardonnay, Riesling, Viognier

Coffee   Sherry, Tawny Port, Grenache

Corn   Chardonnay, sparkling wine, Pinot Gris

Crab   Riesling, Chardonnay, Chenin Blanc

Cream   Chardonnay, sparkling wine, late harvest white wines

Cucumber   Riesling, Sauvignon Blanc

Curry   Riesling, Gewürztraminer, Zinfandel

Dill   Sauvignon Blanc, Sémillon, Riesling

Duck   Gewürztraminer, Riesling, Pinot Noir, Merlot

Egg   Cava, Blanc de Blancs Champagne, Pinot Blanc, dry rosés, unoaked Chardonnay, aged white wines

Eggplant   Tannic wines, Sangiovese, dry rosés

Fennel   Sauvignon Blanc, Pinot Gris/Grigio, Grüner Veltliner, Pinot Noir

Fig   Tawny Port, Vin Santo, Madeira

Fish, pink   Dry rosés, Pinot Noir, Chardonnay, sparkling rosés

Fish, white   Pinot Gris/Grigio, Albariño, sparkling wine, unoaked Chardonnay, Riesling, Pinot Noir

Garlic   Sauvignon Blanc, dry rosés, Chardonnay, Zinfandel

Ginger   Gewürztraminer, Riesling, Viognier

Grapefruit   Sauvignon Blanc, sparkling wine

Green beans   Grüner Veltliner, Gewürztraminer

Halibut   *See* Fish, white

Ham   *See* Pork

Hazelnut   *See* Nuts

Herbes de Provence   Riesling, French Sauvignon Blanc, Sémillon, Sangiovese, French Pinot Noir, dry rosés

Honey   Late harvest white wines, Chenin Blanc, aged Pinot Gris, Riesling, Syrah

Horseradish   Rosé Champagne, Gewürztraminer, Zinfandel

Hummus   Dry rosés, Pinot Gris/Grigio, Pinot Noir

Lamb   Pinot Noir, dry rosés, Syrah/Shiraz, Tempranillo, Zinfandel, Cabernet Franc

Lemon   Sauvignon Blanc, Riesling, Sauternes

Lime   Sauvignon Blanc, Riesling, late harvest white wine

Liver   Late harvest white wine, French Pinot Noir, Syrah, Tempranillo

Lobster   Chardonnay, sparkling wine, Riesling, Rhone white, Pinot Noir

Mango   Riesling, unoaked Chardonnay, late harvest white wine

Maple   Sparkling Shiraz, Riesling, Viognier

Mayonnaise   Chardonnay, sparkling wine

Melon   Chardonnay, Pinot Gris/Grigio, demi-sec Champagne

Mint   Sauvignon Blanc, Cabernet Sauvignon

Mushrooms   Pinot Noir, Madeira, Chardonnay, sparkling wine, Tempranillo, Zinfandel

Mussels   Sauvignon Blanc, Viognier, Albariño

Mustard   Unoaked Chardonnay, Pinot Noir, Zinfandel

Nutmeg   Chardonnay, Pinot Noir

Nuts   Sherry, dry Madeira, Tawny Port, tannic red wines, Chardonnay

Olives   Sherry, dry rosés, Albariño, Tempranillo

Onion   Pinot Blanc, Pinot Grigio/Gris, Riesling, Beaujolais, Syrah

Orange   Riesling, sparkling wine, Syrah/Shiraz, Grenache

Oregano   Sauvignon Blanc, Sangiovese

Oysters   Sparkling wine, unoaked Chardonnay

Paprika   Riesling, Zinfandel

Pâté   *See* Liver

Peach   Riesling, Chenin Blanc, sparkling wine, late harvest white wines, Vin Santo

Peanut   *See* Nuts

Pear   Riesling, Gewürztraminer, late harvest white wines, sparkling wine

Peas   Sauvignon Blanc

Pecans   *See* Nuts

Pepper, ground black and pink   Gewürztraminer, Cabernet Sauvignon, Syrah/Shiraz, Zinfandel

Pepper, ground white   Gewürztraminer, Viognier, Rhone reds

Pineapple   Riesling, late harvest white wines

Polenta   Chardonnay, Blanc de Blancs Champagne

Pork   Riesling, Gewürztraminer, Pinot Blanc, Chardonnay, Pinot Noir, Rhone reds, Zinfandel

Potato   Chardonnay, sparkling wine

Raisin   Late harvest wines

Rice   Pinot Gris/Grigio, Riesling, Albariño, Chardonnay, sparkling wine

Rosemary   Riesling, Sauvignon Blanc, Cabernet Sauvignon, Cabernet Franc

Saffron   Chardonnay, dry rosés, Cabernet Franc

Sage   Riesling, red wines

Salmon   *See* Fish, pink

Salt   Sparkling wine, Riesling, Zinfandel

Sausage   Riesling, Beaujolais, Zinfandel, Sangiovese, Pinotage

Scallops   Riesling, Blanc de Blancs Champagne, Albariño, Chardonnay

Sesame   Chardonnay, Viognier, Riesling

Shrimp   Sauvignon Blanc, Albariño, dry rosés, Pinot Noir

Smoke   Sparkling wine, Chardonnay, Sherry, Pinot Noir, Zinfandel

Soy sauce   Gewürztraminer, Pinot Noir, dry rosés

Spinach   Unoaked Chardonnay, Sauvignon Blanc, Beaujolais

Squash   Viognier, Madeira, Sherry, French Sauvignon Blanc, Beaujolais

Sweet potato   Demi-sec Champagne, Chardonnay, Gewürztraminer, late harvest white wines

Swordfish   *See* Fish, white

Tarragon   Sauvignon Blanc, unoaked Chardonnay, Merlot, Cabernet Franc

Thyme   Sauvignon Blanc, Cabernet Sauvignon, Sangiovese, Rhone reds, dry rosés

Tomato   Albariño, Sauvignon Blanc, Sangiovese, Tempranillo, dry rosés

Trout   *See* Fish, white

Tuna   *See* Fish, pink

Turkey   Chardonnay, Gewürztraminer, Pinot Noir, Beaujolais, dry rosés

Vanilla   Sparkling wine, Chardonnay, oaked wines

Veal   Chardonnay, Pinot Noir, aged reds

Vinegar   Sauvignon Blanc, Riesling, Pinot Noir, Tempranillo

Walnut   *See* Nuts

Yogurt   Riesling, sparkling wines, Chardonnay

Zucchini   Sauvignon Blanc, Sangiovese

The Least You Need to Know

◆ How you cook a food changes its flavors and pairing options.

◆ Examine the qualities of basic ingredients before pairing.

◆ Rubs and seasonings will affect pairings.

◆ Consider the predominant flavors of a dish before pairing, and remember that the predominant flavors can come from spices, oils, and other secondary ingredients.

Chapter 8

Sauce and Side Dish Pairings

In This Chapter

- ◆ Pairing goals for sauces
- ◆ Adding wine to sauces
- ◆ Pairing to side dishes
- ◆ Solving the Thanksgiving pairing conundrum
- ◆ Great pairs for great sauces

To properly pair a sauce, you first need to determine your goal for the pairing. In the following pages you will learn how to set your sauce pairing goals and find out when and why you might want to pair to a sauce instead of the entrée itself. To make the pairing process even easier, you will find a list of suggested wine pairings for classical and not-so-classical sauces.

Although it's most common to pair wine with main entrées and proteins, sometimes the best pairing opportunities come from the side dishes. And side dishes are never more important than at the Thanksgiving table. In addition to helping you with the pairing conundrum posed by Thanksgiving, this chapter offers some general rules for pairing wines with other holiday meals, as well as with side dishes in general.

Setting Your Goals for Sauce Pairings

Having your pairing goals in mind is particularly important when dealing with sauces.

When pairing a dish that is accompanied by a sauce, your first task is to determine whether you want to pair with the sauce or the food. You might decide to pair with the sauce because the sauce is special—your grandmother's special gravy, for example. You might also pair to the sauce because the sauce is more interesting or intense than what it covers—broiled chicken or boiled pasta noodles in a rich cream sauce, for example. A third reason to pair to the sauce is because the wine you are serving better matches up with the sauce flavorings than the entrée itself.

Once you've decided to pair to the sauce, rather than to the entrée, you need to decide if you want the wine to …

◆ Match or mimic the flavors of the sauce.

◆ Enhance and amplify those flavors.

◆ Cut through the sauce.

Consider pan-seared scallops topped with a rich, brown butter sauce. Do you want a wine that mimics that richness, or a wine that cuts through the richness? If the former is your goal, look for a buttery, oaked Chardonnay; if the latter is your goal, try a French Chardonnay with high acidity and body, like Chablis, which cuts through the butter.

If you're serving filet mignon with a peppercorn sauce, decide how much of that peppery flavor you want to bring out. If you want to highlight the pepper, you might choose a Shiraz. Otherwise, you might pick a California Cabernet Sauvignon. Choosing a goal gives you direction, and it sets the tone of the pairing.

Wine Nerd

One of the best quotes about wine and sauces comes from *The Standard Wine Book*. This book, in quoting an old edition of *Encyclopaedia Britannica*, says "Wine at the table promotes appetite, digestion, and well-being. Saucelike, it accents the flavors of food." And, as we know, it also accents the flavor of sauces, too.

Getting Sauced: Adding Wine to Sauces

People have been adding wine to sauces for as long as they've been making sauces. Wine is a staple ingredient in a number of classic sauces, including bourguignon, beurre blanc, and many marinaras. Who hasn't tippled a little wine into that canned spaghetti sauce to give it a little more oomph?

When used correctly, wine adds a depth of flavor to sauces. The aromas of wine add their nuances to sauces, and they can also bring out other flavors in the sauce. Because they have such a large impact on the sauces, it's important to use a good wine when cooking.

Because cheap wine typically is unbalanced, if you add it to a sauce, then you will likely have to add more sugar, spices, or salt to balance out the sauce's flavors. That's why you should never cook with wine you wouldn't drink by itself.

Corked

Never add cooking wine to sauces. Not only is it usually made from bad wine, but it also contains additives and salt, which can adversely affect the dish or sauce. Cheap wine can do the same thing.

Fine restaurants actually use good-quality wine in the kitchen. Chefs typically use wine that is a day or two old, but it's always good-quality wine—the wine that is served by the glass in the restaurant.

If you are planning to serve a particular wine with your dinner and your sauce calls for adding wine, add an ounce or two of the wine you're serving. You will still have enough wine to drink at the table, and that great wine will help you turn out a great sauce. Plus, it will pair perfectly!

Now, if you are planning to serve a $200 wine with dinner and you're cooking a dish like *coq au vin* (chicken with wine), which uses almost an entire bottle of wine, you're not going to want to use such an expensive wine in the dish. But don't buy a cheap $5 bottle of swill to use in the recipe. Instead buy a good $10 or $15 bottle of wine that has similar aromas and characteristics as that fabulous bottle you're planning to uncork. You'll have a better pairing, and you'll end up with a better meal overall.

Wine Nerd

If you cook with wine (or beer or spirits), you can still serve that dish to children or others who do not drink alcohol. When you heat wine or other alcoholic beverages, the alcohol cooks off. Now, if you pour wine over your chocolate dessert or add it after the cooking process is complete, the alcohol will still be present in the dish.

Dishing on Side Dish Pairings

Most of the time, wine is paired with the main course or entrée. You don't typically pair wine with potatoes, veggies, or other side dishes. But sometimes, you might want to.

When would you pair wine with a side dish instead of the entrée? When the side dish is more exciting or flavorful than the entrée. Roasted chicken without a sauce is rather boring; but when served with a fantastic side of potatoes au gratin, the chicken becomes more exciting. In addition, the potatoes might be the better match for pairing.

You might also want to pair the wine with the side dish to highlight the dish—for instance, if it is a special recipe that's been in your family for years, or if you just happen to prefer the side dish. Let's say you're serving Grandma's tomato-eggplant casserole with roast beef and mashed potatoes, and your family just loves that casserole. The casserole really is the star of the meal, not the beef; in this case, it makes sense to match the wine with the side, not the entrée.

The same rules for pairing entrées and sauces apply to side dishes: Determine your goals in pairing, pick out the predominant flavors of the dish, and start researching wines.

Things can get complicated if you're trying to pair more than one side dish at a time. In that case, determine the predominant flavors of the dishes.

Perfect Pairings _____

Though you can set up a perfect pairing for mashed potatoes or steamed broccoli, you probably won't want to. Save your side dish pairings for spectacular or personally significant side dishes.

Solving the Thanksgiving Conundrum

Okay, let's get real. Although it might not seem like Thanksgiving without a turkey, Thanksgiving is never just about the turkey. It's about all of those family favorites—mashed potatoes oozing with Grandma's gravy, sweet potatoes buried in butter and brown sugar, green bean and broccoli cheese casseroles, tangy cranberry relish, spiced pumpkin pie … you get the picture.

Thanksgiving, more than any other holiday, is a challenge for pairing. The reason it's so complicated is, well, because it's a complicated meal. Every family has its own Thanksgiving traditions, and those traditions usually involve a lot of different dishes crowding each other on the table.

But it's not just the sheer number of dishes—it's their diversity in flavors, textures, and weights. That's where things really start getting tricky.

One of the most common wines people serve at Thanksgiving is Zinfandel. It's an all-American grape, and well, Thanksgiving is an all-American holiday. Zin boasts a lot of fruit aromas, and it can hold its own against heavy gravies. It's a good option.

Beaujolais Nouveau is another favorite Thanksgiving wine. It's a lighter red, which tends to work better with poultry than heavier, more tannic reds.

Then there is Nouveau's often overlooked big sibling "Cru" Beaujolais. This light, red wine often tastes—and can be drunk—just like French Burgundy. These wines are labeled as "Beaujolais" (sans the "Nouveau") and with their village of origin.

Instead of those ruby colored Beaujolais wines, some people go with an off-dry Riesling or Gewürztraminer, as their sweet fruitiness and acidity work well with the richness and sweetness at the Thanksgiving table.

Zinfandel, Beaujolais Nouveau, Riesling, and Gewürztraminer all work at the Thanksgiving table. But whether you choose any of these varietals or another entirely will depend on your pairing goals.

Do you want to pair to the turkey itself? If so, how do you cook your turkey—Roasted or fried? Stuffed with herbs or just basted with butter? Think of the turkey and how it is cooked, and then think of the predominant flavors in the seasonings you use.

But if your family is just crazy about Aunt Jenna's stuffing or Grandma's green bean casserole, then you might want to pair to those dishes instead. Go with the star of your Thanksgiving meal—whatever that dish may be.

If there are several stars on the table, don't be afraid to open up more than one bottle of wine. You can even turn the Thanksgiving table into a mini wine-tasting event.

> **Wine Nerd**
>
> Beaujolais wines hail from one of 10 villages, but our favorites hail from Moulin-à-Vent and Fleurie. Whether Nouveau or Cru, all Beaujolais comes from the Gamay grape, in a region within the southern tip of Burgundy.

> **Perfect Pairings**
>
> If you drown your turkey, mashed potatoes, and stuffing with a heavy gravy, pair to the gravy, not the turkey. And for an easy, perfect pairing, add a little wine to the gravy before serving.

Follow the same suggestions for other holiday meals. Pick out the star of the meal, set your goals for pairing, and have fun.

Time to Get Pairing

Now that you understand how to pair side dishes and sauces, you're ready to get pairing. For some extra help, Jaclyn has put together a master list of more than 20 sauces and the wines that go with them.

Alfredo sauce   Chardonnay, Pinot Gris/Grigio, Prosecco

Asian chili sauce   A sweeter white like Riesling or Chenin Blanc

Barbeque   Riesling, Shiraz, Zinfandel

Béarnaise   Chardonnay, sparkling wine, Pinot Gris/Grigio

Beurre blanc   White wine that was used to make the sauce; sparkling wine

Beurre rouge   Red wine that was used to make the sauce

Bolognese   Sangiovese, Cabernet Sauvignon, Zinfandel

Brown butter sauce   Oaked Chardonnay, sparkling wine

Caramel sauce   Madeira, Tawny Port, Sauternes

Cheese sauce   Pinot Grigio, Chardonnay, sparkling wine, Pinot Noir, Merlot

Chocolate sauce   Madeira, Tokaji, Sherry, Vin Santo

Gravy   Off-dry Gewürztraminer, Pinot Noir, Zinfandel, demi-sec Champagne, sparkling Shiraz

Hollandaise   Sparkling wine, oaked Chardonnay, French Sauvignon Blanc

Pesto   Grüner Veltliner, Sauvignon Blanc, Pinot Grigio

Marinara   Sangiovese, Tempranillo, Sauvignon Blanc, dry rosé

Mole   Zinfandel, Shiraz, off-dry Riesling

Mushroom sauce   Madeira, Pinot Noir, Blanc de Noirs Champagne

Mustard sauce   Unoaked Chardonnay, Pinot Noir, Zinfandel

Peanut sauce   Off-dry Riesling, oaked Chardonnay, Pinot Noir

Romesco   Albariño, Chardonnay, Tempranillo

Salsa   Albariño, off-dry Riesling, Tempranillo

Sweet and sour sauce   Off-dry Gewürztraminer, off-dry Riesling

Teriyaki sauce   Off-dry Riesling, off-dry Gewürztraminer, Pinot Noir, Zinfandel

Tzatziki   Dry rosé, Pinot Gris/Grigio

The Least You Need to Know

◆ When pairing wines with sauces, first decide whether to match the sauce or to balance it out.

◆ When cooking with wine, use a good-quality wine.

◆ Pair with side dishes if they are more interesting or intensely flavored than the main course.

◆ Four good wines for the Thanksgiving table are Zinfandel, Beaujolais, Riesling, and Gewürztraminer.

◆ Pair with the "star" of your holiday meal, which is not always the main entrée.

Part 3

Putting It Back Together: Pairing Principles

Once you understand the basics of wine and food pairing, the principles of pairing are a cinch. This part shows you how to take the concepts outlined in Part 2 to the next level. You'll explore pairing principles such as "Red goes with red and white goes with white" and "Goes with where it grows." You will also learn how to pair by science, as well as by intuition, and you'll even get some insights on pairing international cuisines with wine and experimenting with pairings.

9

Red Goes with Red, White Goes with White

In This Chapter

- ◆ Why red wines work with red meats
- ◆ Why white wines work with white meats
- ◆ Where pink wines fit in
- ◆ When to break the rules

Red goes with red, white goes with white. This is the one wine-pairing rule that even the least wine-savvy among us know. But while most of us have followed this rule, many of us don't understand why it works.

In this chapter you will get some insight into the philosophy behind the pairing rule, and see why it applies even to nonmeat foods.

But as the old saying goes, rules are made to be broken. And that goes for the red-with-red, white-with-white rule, too.

The Easiest Rule in Wine Pairing

The golden rule of wine pairing is as follows: Pair red wines with red meats; pair white wines with white meats. It's a simple, traditional rule, along the lines of "never wear white shoes after Labor Day." But while we've largely abandoned coordinating our shoe color with the seasons, we haven't abandoned the wine color rule.

And with good reason; when something works, you stick with it. The basic principles of pairing explain why this time honored wine-pairing rule works, red meats need heavier, more intense wines, while white meats need lighter, less intense wines. Obviously, there's a little more to it than that, but not much.

The reason people have "always" paired white wines with white meats and red wines with red meats is that, historically, this pairing developed in wine-producing regions. The terroir, which will be discussed more fully in Chapter 10, not only produced wines, but it also produced cuisines, and the wines and cuisines grew up together.

It just so happened that many white wine–producing regions of the world also happened to have access to fish or poultry (the Loire Valley and its Sauvignon Blanc–based wines, for example, pair fabulously with local river fish), and the same is true for red wine regions having access to red meats.

While terroir might explain the origins of this rule, it doesn't explain why it became "the wine rule." It became the wine rule in the 1970s and 1980s, right around the time when American winemakers were just gaining exposure and furthering the qualities of their production. As wine grew in popularity, the rule became even more entrenched.

> ### Wine Nerd
>
> American wine producers gained international acclaim in 1976 when wine merchant, Steven Spurrier organized a blind tasting of American wines versus French wines. The Americans trumped the French in what has become known as "the Judgment of Paris." The same vintages were tasted again in blind competition in 1986 and in 2006, and in both subsequent competitions, the American wines aged better, trumping the French each time. The movie *Bottle Shock*, tells the story of the competition in a fun, exaggerated, Hollywood sort of way.

By the 1980s and 1990s, this rule became established even more. But in the advent of the modern wine dinner, many sommeliers and chefs have made a concerted, conscious effort to break this rule. Sometimes, the rule has been broken to great effect, while other times, it has resulted in silly pairs.

Why the Rule Works

Red wines work with red meats mainly because their intensity levels match. Delicate, light whites just don't stand up to hearty stews or big steaks.

The heavy tannins in reds stand up to the umami flavors in meats, and they also have the stronger, heavier bodies and mouthfeels that match the heavier weights of the meats.

Lighter, white meats, on the other hand, can be overwhelmed and drowned out by heavier, red wines. A delicate seafood soufflé will be overpowered by a heavy Cabernet Sauvignon. The tannins mask the flavors and the nuances of white meats and seafoods. In both cases, it's a question of balance and enhancement. When you pair wines with foods, you want them to enhance—not overpower—one another.

But you should know by now that just because a wine is red, doesn't mean it will be a perfect pairing for red meat. Conversely, just because a wine is white, doesn't mean that it will be a perfect pairing for white meats. When pairing according to this principle, the key is to match intensity.

As you have learned, not all reds are created equal. The same goes for whites. For a heavy, charred steak, you want a heavy, charred wine, and a Beaujolais Nouveau is not going to cut it. For a rich, buttery chicken à la king, a delicate, just released Pinot Gris isn't going to work, either.

There's a progression of intensity with red wines and white wines. With red wines, Pinot Noir and Beaujolais wines are on the lighter end of the spectrum, with Cabernet Sauvignons and Syrahs on the heavier end. With white

> **Perfect Pairings**
>
> Always try to match the intensity of the wine with the intensity of the dish. Not all reds or whites match with red or white meats.

Perfect Pairings

The color rule also applies to sauces. White sauces go with white wines while red sauces go with red wines. Alfredo, beurre blanc, and mayonnaise all work better with white wines. Mushroom, barbecue, and tomato sauces all work better with red wines.

wines, Pinot Gris and Rieslings are on the lighter side while aged, heavily oaked Chardonnays are on the heavier side.

The same is true of meats: chicken, delicate fish (like tilapia and orange roughy), and seafood (like scallops and crab) are all on the lighter side. Shrimp, game birds (like duck and goose), salmon, and pork, fall in the middle of the spectrum. Meats like steak, lamb, and game meats all qualify as heavy foods.

Pink Is in the Middle

Just like the pink in the middle signifies a perfectly prepared, medium-rare steak, pink wines, or rosés, are in the middle of the pairing spectrum.

This means that rosés pair perfectly with pink meats. Pork dishes, ham, smoked chicken, and salmon all go great with rosés. Ahi tuna and red snapper go with rosés, too. And pink sauces—tomato cream, for example—also pair splendidly with rosés.

Rosés can act as a bridge wine for pairings on both sides. If someone generally prefers white wines, but they're eating a steak, a rosé would work much better than a Riesling. Conversely, if you prefer reds, but you're gnawing on a chicken leg, a rosé will work better than a Tempranillo.

When to Break the Rule

Recently, sommeliers and chefs have made a concerted effort to break the color rule—sometimes to great effect. It all really comes down to your pairing goals for a dish. If you're pairing to a sauce rather than to the meat itself, it might make sense to violate the rule. Same goes for if you're pairing to a side dish rather than to the main entrée.

So if you really want to pair a red wine with chicken or a white wine with steak, think about sauces, think about spices, think about what other ingredients are in the dish. You can use spices, sauces, and garnishes to transition wines and meats that aren't automatic pairs.

Peppercorns and mushrooms are two ingredients that immediately pair better with red wines; same goes for cream and butter with white wines. Barbecue sauce, for example, whether it is added to chicken, shrimp, or pork, almost always pairs well with a fruity Zinfandel. Alfredo sauce almost always pairs well with Chardonnay. For more specific ideas on pairing wines to sauces, check Chapter 8's list of pairings.

Also, keep the intensity of the dish in mind. If you are intent on pairing a red wine with a light fish dish, don't pour a big Cab. Instead, look to a Beaujolais, a Pinot Noir, or a Tempranillo. And if you just have to drink a white wine with your steak, stay away from Sauvignon Blanc, and steer yourself towards an oaky Chardonnay.

If you adhere to the basic wine-pairing principles, you'll probably come up with some good pairings. And remember, ultimately it all comes down to personal preference.

Wine Nerd

In *The Frugal Gourmet Cooks with Wine,* Father Corbet Clark wrote the chapter on pairing. Fr. Clark's number one rule? "Drink the wines you enjoy with the foods you enjoy. You have a thirst for Riesling and a hunger for steak? So be it. You will not be zapped with lightning for putting the two together." Amen to that!

The Least You Need to Know

- ◆ Red wine goes with red meat and white wine goes with white meat because their intensities match.

- ◆ Red sauces go with red wines, and white sauces go with white wines.

- ◆ Pink or rosé wines go with pink foods like salmon and pork.

- ◆ Pink wines can also be served with both red and white meats.

- ◆ If you want to serve red wine with white meat or white wine with red meat, think about intensity, and use sauces, spices, and additions to transition the wine to the food.

10

Pairing by Terroir

In This Chapter

- ◆ Understanding terroir
- ◆ Old-World vs. New-World wine-making
- ◆ New-World terroirs
- ◆ Pairing suggestions

You already know from Chapter 1 that a wine's terroir—a catch-all term describing the geography, weather, soil-type, and other conditions where a wine grape is grown—influences a wine's taste and aroma. A Chardonnay grown in California tastes far different than a Chardonnay grown in France. California Chardonnays typically have tropical fruit flavors, such as pineapple and melon, while French Chardonnays are more citrusy and minerally.

Terroir applies just as well to foods grown in a particular region; for instance, a British cheddar tastes completely different from a Canadian cheddar. The milk, the aging methods, what the cows eat, and even the bacteria in the air all affect the resulting tastes.

If you don't know what wine to pair with a dish, look to the dish's origins and pick a wine from that region. "Goes with where it grows" is a very simple wine-pairing rule, and it is an easy one to fall back on.

Understanding Terroir

Which came first, the cuisine or the wine? The answer: the cuisine came first. Historically, cuisines and regional foods developed in Europe before wines came along. The wines that came along were developed and honed to match the local cuisines.

Some of the most ancient vineyards are in Greece and, to this day, Greek wines tend to go really well with olives, Feta, and phyllo-wrapped tasty treats. Greek wines were created to match perfectly with Greek cuisine, and elevate the enjoyment of each. But it's not just the Greek who have mastered terroir pairing.

def•i•ni•tion

Old-World wines are wines originating in Europe. New-World wines are wines from the United States, Canada, Argentina, Chile, Australia, and New Zealand.

The *Old-World wines* of Europe tend to match their region's cuisines. The wines of France, Italy, Spain, Germany, Austria, and Portugal were all specially crafted and formulated to go with the foods of their regions. Now, this does not mean that all Italian wines are great with Piedmont's rich, truffle-filled dishes. Quite the contrary.

Instead, you must further narrow the scope by focusing on wine from that specific region. Nebbiolo- and Dolcetto-based wines from the Piedmont region are perfect with the food grown in that part of the country. Not only have the wine-making traditions helped the wine pair well with regional dishes, but the fact that food crops and pastures share the soil with nearby grapes seems to magically create shared notes and characteristics within the wines. In Piedmont, for example, the wines often have an aroma reminiscent of the truffles that are harvested nearby.

Wine is very region-specific throughout Europe. So much so that special government agencies have been created to make sure that winemakers are required by law to uphold certain traditions within each region. In the region of Chianti Classico, for example, winemakers must make their wines with at least 80 percent Sangiovese, those wines must have at least 12.5 percent alcohol, and they must age it for a minimum of seven months in oak. Such strict guidelines may sound very limiting, but they ensure quality and consistency. When you buy a Chianti Classico, you have a very good sense of what the wine is going to taste like. The good news for pairing purposes is that such consistency makes it a breeze to pair these wines with foods from the region.

Europe's Wine-Making Regions

Every wine-making country breaks its land into specific wine-making areas known as *appellations*. In the Old World these appellations are far more defined and regulated than in the *New World*.

For a wine to be considered a Bordeaux, for example, the winemaker has to adhere to very specific wine-making techniques and traditions, and only grapes grown in Bordeaux are certified as coming from that appellation. Each country has a slightly different way to referring to their appellations. Here are the major Old-World appellations, by country:

◆ **France** Appellation d'Origine Contrôlée (AOC, or sometimes, just AC). France has 10 major wine-making regions, and within those regions there are more than 100 smaller regions, each with its own unique terroirs. For more information, check out www. terroir-france.com.

def•i•ni•tion

Appellations are very specific geographical locations for making wines.

◆ **Italy** Denominazione di Origine Controllata (DOC). Italy has 20 major wine-making regions.

◆ **Spain** Denominación de Origen Calificada (DOC) as well as Denominación de Origen (DO) for region-specific wines. Spain has only two DOC regions—Rioja and Priorat—but it has 60 different DO regions. DOC is more highly regulated than DO.

◆ **Portugal** Denominacção de Origem (DOC). Portugal currently has 19 major wine-making regions.

A Few Words about Table Wines

Any European wines that aren't labeled with a specific appellation such as AOC, DOC, or DO are considered *table wines.* Some European winemakers produce some mighty fine table wines, so don't write these wines off. More and more Old-World winemakers are moving away from tradition and experimenting with different varietals and wine-making techniques. So when you see a lack of appellation on the label or the words "table wine," read the back label, or talk to your neighborhood wine shop owner or favorite somme-lier, to find out more about the wine.

def•i•ni•tion

Table wine is simply a wine that isn't labeled with a specific appellation.

Because Europe has such stringent wine-making standards, you pretty much know what kind of wine you're going to get from each appel-lation. It is going to be very terroir-driven, meaning that it will have aromas from its environment. In Burgundian red wines, you will often detect a note of "forest floor" on the nose. This earthy, mineral aroma pairs beautifully with mushrooms and dried herbs. You shouldn't be surprised to learn that Burgundy is known for its mushrooms. When you sample an Albariño from the coastal regions of Spain, you may detect some salt water aromas, making it a great accompaniment with seafood. Again, Galicia, the region where Albariño is predominantly grown, is known for its seafood.

The Science of Terroir

Scientists are still trying to figure out why terroir—the geography, soil-type, and climate—affects wines the way it does. Almost every year a new study comes out that "definitively" explains terroir, but then almost immediately another study comes out to contradict the first one. What we do know is that soil conditions play a huge role in wines, and that soil is a prominent characteristic of terroir.

For one thing, only certain grapes can be grown in certain soils, and certain climates have very specific effects on grapes. Sunlight, or lack thereof, also has an effect on grapes. Some grapes need more sunlight than others to ripen. Petit Verdot, for example, can only be grown in warm areas that have a very long ripening season, otherwise the grapes will never ripen. So planting Petit Verdot in Germany, with its cooler climate, would be foolish. Think of it as putting a fresh-water fish in a salt-water tank. Certain grapes are just built for certain terroirs.

So what does terroir have to do with pairing? First, if you know what a wine's aromas are most likely going to be, then you'll be able to pair it better. Second, these wines will most likely pair well with cuisines from the same regions.

Sauvignon Blanc from Sancerre, located in France's Loire Valley, goes great with the pork and chicken terrines from that region. And the Tempranillo-based reds of Spain's Rioja region go great with Manchego cheese and Spanish chorizo.

> **Wine Nerd**
>
> One of the weirdest things about terroir is that even ground cover plants can affect the taste of grapes. For example, grapes grown adjacent to lavender or mustard plants can take on the aromas of those plants. Scientists still don't know exactly why this is the case and they continue to study the phenomenon.

That means if you are planning to serve a Tuscan bean soup, you might want to look to its wine-neighbor, Chianti, for pairing. If you're making some Andalusian tapas, pair them up with a variety of Sherries. Planning a hearty German dinner? Look to Germany's Spätburgunder and Riesling wines.

Old-World Wine-Making vs. New-World Wine-Making

Up to this point we've been talking specifically about Old-World wines. It's not that the United States and other New-World wine-making regions, like Australia or New Zealand, aren't influenced by their terroirs. They are. A Pinot Noir produced in the Alexander Valley in Sonoma County is going to be quite different from one developed in the Willamette Valley of Oregon or Burgundy, France.

Terroir does play an important role in wine-making in the United States, and you can taste it, just as you can taste the terroirs of Europe.

Wine Nerd

One of the newest AVAs in the United States is also the country's largest: the Upper Mississippi Valley AVA, which encompasses about 30,000 square miles in Wisconsin, Minnesota, Iowa, and Illinois. Having this AVA designation will help these Midwestern wineries market their wines better. We hope it produces better wine, too, but that's no guarantee.

But although the United States has its European counterpart of appellations, called the American Viticultural Area (AVA) designation, our winemakers don't have to adhere to stringent rules. If a winemaker wants to age his Cabernet Sauvignon in new oak and then blend it with stainless steel–fermented Chardonnay, he can go ahead and do it. If a winemaker wants to make her Shiraz sparkling, she can go ahead and do it. And, unlike in Old-World wine-making countries, winemakers are not limited to growing only certain types of grapes in their AVA.

While you can taste the terroir in New-World wines, terroir isn't the final word on how wines are made in countries like the United States, New Zealand, Chile, Argentina, South Africa, and Australia. American and Australian winemakers, in particular, tend to be quite creative, and they're driven by their grapes, their tastes, and their own personal quirks, instead of their region's traditions and terroir.

A Chardonnay from chalk-rich soil in California may show some chalky notes in the nose if it was traditionally fermented and aged. However, the winemakers have the freedom to ferment that Chardonnay in all new oak which will overrule the terroir-driven nose and, instead, create a rich, nutty smelling wine. They can also ferment it in a way that amplifies the fruit aromas. This free-for-all approach to wine-making means that wines from a single New-World region vary greatly from vintner to vintner.

Wine Nerd

Because Americans love to drink these crazy, experimental wines, and because Americans' love of wine grows each year, more European winemakers want to hone in on this growing market. Spanish and Italian winemakers, in particular, are growing more and more creative. For some crazy wines, check out wines from southern France and "Super Tuscan" wines from Italy.

Because all this experimentation is going on in New-World wines, you can't rely on pairing by region. Napa Valley wines, for example, don't all pair up perfectly with California cuisine. Instead, with most New-World wines, you have to rely on pairing by wine-making style and dominate characteristics of each individual wine, as discussed in previous chapters. South America and New Zealand are known for specifically crafting wines to go with the local cuisine, even though most winemakers blend traditional and New-World wine-making techniques. For example, Argentinean Cabernet Sauvignons and Malbecs have very distinctive, green pepper aromas and rich tannins, making them great with the meaty, rustic, barbecue dishes and chimichurri sauces that characterize Argentinian or Gaucho cuisines.

Chilean wines also go really well with Chilean cuisines. Chile is known for its seafood, and its Sauvignon Blancs go fabulously with Chilean sea bass. Chilean Carménère wines also go well with Chilean stews. And New Zealand's famous lamb pairs deliciously with a New Zealand Pinot Noir.

> **Wine Nerd**
>
> Argentina is the fifth largest wine-producing region in the world, after France, Italy, Spain, and the United States. Australia holds down sixth place.

Applying the Terroir Rule

If you are trying to pair an Old-World wine with food, look to the cuisines of the region the wine hails from. Here's a short list of terroir-based pairings:

Dish/Ingredient	Where It Originates	What It Goes With
Dijon mustard	Burgundy, France	Burgundian Chardonnay or Pinot Noir (depending on the dish's intensity)
Escargot	Burgundy, France	Burgundian Chardonnay
Tarte tatin (Apple tart)	Loire Valley, France	Sweet Chenin Blanc
Black truffle risotto	Piedmont, Italy	Nebbiolo, especially Barolo and Barbaresco

continues

continued

Dish/Ingredient	Where It Originates	What It Goes With
Pesto	Liguria, Italy	Vermentino-based white wine
Sauerkraut	Alsace, France; Germany	Dry Alsatian Pinot Gris, Pinot Blanc, Sylvaner, Gewürztraminer, dry German Riesling
Paella	Valencia, Spain	Tempranillo, Moscatel, or Monastrell-based wines; Spanish Viognier or rosé
Pasta e fagioli (Italian bean and pasta soup)	Veneto, Italy	Valpolicella or Amarone
Foie gras	Bordeaux and Alsace, France	Sauternes, Pinot Gris, and Alsatian Gewürztraminer
Empanadas	Galicia, Spain, Portugal; South America	Albariño and dry Portuguese white wines, Tempranillo, South American reds
Asado (roasted meat)	Argentina, Chile, Uruguay	Chilean Merlot and Cabernet Sauvignon, Argentinian Malbec, Uruguayan Tannat
Colonial goose (roasted lamb leg dish)	New Zealand	New Zealand Pinot Noir
Wiener schnitzel	Vienna, Austria	Austrian Grüner Veltliner
Lamb gyros	Macedonia, Greece	Xinomavro and other Greek red wines.
Pizza	Campania, Italy	Aglianico-based reds, especially Taurasi

If you are planning to make a region- or country-specific meal, in addition to looking to that region or country's wines, you can also look for wines that are labeled as "made in the style of." Pinot Noirs, for example, "made in a Burgundian style," might not have the exact earthy aromas as those that come from Burgundy, but they will not be as fruity or intense as other Pinot Noirs.

You can also look to pair dishes by terroir, based on specific ingredients. For instance, most dishes featuring Spanish paprika will likely pair beautifully with a Tempranillo. If you are using imported Italian tomatoes and imported Italian cheeses, try a Chianti.

> **Perfect Pairings**
>
> Don't just pair by terroir for the dish as a whole. You can pair by terroir when using ingredients that are the prominent flavors of a dish.

The Least You Need to Know

◆ Most European wine-making focuses on terroir.

◆ You know an Old-World wine is true to its terroir if it is labeled AOC, DOC, or DO.

◆ The easiest way to pair by terroir is to pair a wine with food that is common to the region where the wine is cultivated.

◆ Though America and Australia have distinctive terroirs, their winemakers aren't restricted to terroir-based rules and regulations.

◆ South American and New Zealand wines tend to go well with South American and New Zealand dishes.

Chapter 11

The Science of Pairing: Intensity, Acidity, and Sweetness

In This Chapter

- The "science" of pairings
- Pairing by intensity
- Pairing by acidity
- Pairing by sweetness

Though we usually just "like what we like" and "dislike what we dislike," very often, there are measurable reasons for our preferences, and this is definitely the case when it comes to pairing wine with food.

This chapter hones in on the measurable characteristics of wine—its intensity, acid, and sweetness—which influence how well it pairs with food. You'll find out how these characteristics affect a food's taste, and how to use them to your advantage when you are pairing wine with food.

Understanding the "Science" of Pairings

Although wine and food pairings aren't rocket science, it is possible to pair by measurable characteristics. So when we say we're pairing by science, what we're really pairing by are the measurable characteristics of wine and food.

While it's sometimes hard to quantify why we like or dislike a particular wine or food, other times it's quite straightforward. For example, if a chef was heavy-handed with the salt shaker, it's pretty easy to say you dislike a dish because it was too salty. It's equally easy to say you dislike a wine because it was corked.

Similarly, it makes perfect sense to say that you like a dish or a wine because it is well-balanced, meaning that its flavors all tend to add up in the right proportions. If any particular characteristic is out of proportion, chances are you're not going to like the taste of it.

Like Likes Like

The first measurable rule for pairings is this: intensity likes intensity, acid likes acid, sweetness likes sweetness. In other words, like likes like.

While intensity, acid, and sweetness all affect pairings in a myriad of ways, the most basic rule in considering them is to match them up as closely as you can.

Try pairing up a rich, buttery Chardonnay with a lightly broiled filet of tilapia, and the richness of the wine will be lost on the delicate fish. It doesn't add up. But if you substitute the tilapia for a steaming bowl of creamy New England clam chowder, you've got the right match for intensity.

That same Chardonnay would be lost on a bowl of lime-squeezed ceviche. The acidity in the wine doesn't match the acidity of the dish; a more acidic Sauvignon Blanc would be a better pairing.

Similarly, a syrupy-sweet, late harvest Gewürztraminer would clash with a not-so-sweet pumpkin soup, but it would be divine with a sweet pumpkin cheesecake.

All About Intensity

Probably the most important pairing characteristic of wine and food is intensity. Intensity is the combined effects of sweetness, tannins, body, alcohol content, and the overall flavors of the wine. People sometimes confuse intensity with the weight of a wine, but it is the overall strength and your perception of the power of the wine.

An intense wine has more alcohol, more tannins, more body, more "oomph." It needs to be paired with food that has more flavor, more strength, more weight.

Almost every pairing principle in some way relates to intensity. The reason chicken and fish pair up nicely with white wines? Intensity. The reason red wines go well with game? Intensity.

If you look at traditional terroir pairings, the intensity of a regional cuisine tends to match the intensity of the regional wines. The cuisine of the Loire Valley is lighter than that of Burgundy, and so are the wines.

If you look at almost any good pairing, you'll see that the intensity of the food and the intensity of the wine match. Meat, for example, offers more intense and more robust flavors than chicken. It's heartier fare, and thus, it needs a heartier wine to match in a pairing.

Perfect Pairings

You will need stronger everything—flavor, weight, and body—in food when pairing with a more intense wine.

Alcohol Content

When defining the intensity of a wine, the first thing to look at is the alcohol content. The higher the alcohol content, the greater the intensity. Alcohol affects wine in two ways: it can make a wine seem "hot" and it can cause fruit notes to be perceived as stronger and jammier.

Perfect Pairings

Typically, the higher the alcohol content, the less sweet the wine will be. Fortified wines are the exception to this guideline; due to their high alcohol content and overall flavor, they are very intense wines.

Body

Typically, wines with a higher alcohol content have a heavier body. Body is the weight of a wine on your palate, and definitely affects food pairings. With body, you can pair like-with-like or go against the grain.

When going with an opposing pairing, it is important that the food be the heavier of the pair. For example, you could pair a heavy Chardonnay with a rich cream sauce for a like-with-like, full-bodied pairing. But if you want to contrast the heaviness of the cream sauce, you could pair it with a crisp Pinot Grigio. You would never want to pair that same Chardonnay with a delicate lemon sauce, as the richness of the wine would overpower the sauce.

Tannins

When pairing foods with red wine, it is important to also note the tannins. Tannins can make a wine seem far more powerful and intense, even if its alcohol and body are lighter. Tannins in wine like tannins in food. Tannins can be found in foods like meats, especially when grilled, bitter greens like kale, and vegetables like eggplant. Wines with tannins also need more richness or fat to cling to. Overall, tannins need food with a higher intensity.

The Spiciness Factor

Every rule has its exceptions, and when it comes to matching intensity, the exception is spicy—as in hot—food. Spicy food should not be paired with an intense wine with a high content of alcohol. When you add more alcohol, you add more heat to a dish. Adding an intense wine to an already spicy dish will overwhelm the palate with spice, and not in a good way.

Corked

Do not pair an intense wine, or a wine with a high alcohol content, with a spicy dish. This will cause sensory overload in the worst possible way.

Instead of pairing spicy food with an intense, alcoholic wine, try pairing it with an intensely sweet and aromatic wine. If the dish is spicy but light, like kung pao chicken, pair it with a sweet, yet delicate wine like Alsatian Pinot Gris. If a dish is spicy and heavy, like Szechwan beef, pair it with a more intense, sweeter wine like Beaujolais.

Understanding Acidity in Pairings

While acidity can help define a wine's intensity, it should be considered in its own right when you pair wine with food. As a general rule acid loves acid. If you've got a dish that has some sourness in it, you're going to want a wine with lots of acid in it.

When considering acid in wine, there are four main types of acid: tartaric, malic, lactic, and citric. All wines have malic, tartaric, and citric acids; but lactic acid is only found in some wines.

Malic, citric, and tartaric acids combine to give wines their puckering, thirst-quenching sensation. Tartaric and malic acids are the most prevalent in grapes, and the higher their levels, the more tart a wine will be. Wines that have a noticeable green apple aroma are higher in malic acid, as this is the aroma most associated with that acid. Wines that have citrus aromas often have higher levels of citric acid.

Lactic acid is created when malic acid transforms into lactic acid by the process of malolactic fermentation. Lactic acid can be found in Chardonnays, and it can also be found in all red wines. This is the acid that gives wine its creamy, round mouthfeel.

Often by identifying the aromas associated with various acids in the nose, you will know what to expect on the palate. All wines contain acids, but wines that have particularly noticeable acids include some Rieslings, Sauvignon Blanc, Pinot Gris, and Barbera. Wines from cooler climates tend to have more of a mouth-puckering quality than wines from warmer climates.

Grapes grown in cooler climates tend to produce a higher acid wine. Acid and sweetness in grapes are inversely related. The more acidic a grape, the less sweet it will be. A

Wine Nerd
Crystals that form at the bottom of a cork, sometimes called wine diamonds, are caused by tartaric acid. These sparkly crystals can be found in both red and white wines. We don't recommend eating them, but they are not harmful and are completely natural.

good way to understand this is if you try to eat an underripe grape, it will taste overwhelmingly tart, whereas if you taste a raisin or a raisinated grape, it will taste super-sweet.

def•i•ni•tion

> **Volatile acidity** or **VA** means the acidity of a wine is so out of balance that it ruins the overall taste of the wine. It is caused by the same bacteria that are used to create vinegar.

In general, acidity in wine is a good thing—so long as it is balanced. When a wine has *volatile acidity (VA)*, it has so much acidity that it is considered flawed. It is quite off-putting, and you definitely know it when you taste it.

Like with Like

When pairing by acidity, try to match the levels of acidity in the wine with the levels of acidity in the food. Acidic food loves acidic wine. That's the reason why fresh chèvre tastes so good with Sauvignon Blanc, and why a Chardonnay would seem bland with such a cheese. The acidity of a chèvre matches the acidity of a Sauvignon Blanc.

Perfect Pairings

> If you are pairing a highly acidic wine like Pinot Grigio or Sauvignon Blanc, squeeze a lemon or a lime over the dish to make it pair up better.

All citrus-spiked sauces and acidic dishes love acidic wines. If you are pairing an acidic wine, sometimes you can just squeeze a lemon or a lime over the dish to make it pair up nicely. This works especially well with chicken, fish and seafood dishes, and it can even work with pork.

Opposites Attract

You can also use the acidity of a wine to cut down on the richness of the dish. Anytime you are looking to cut through the richness or creaminess of a dish, look to an acidic wine to get the job done.

A Pinot Grigio, for example, can be paired with fettuccini Alfredo to cut through the heavy cream. Acidity is also the reason why white wines tend to pair up better with cheeses—the acidity in the wine cuts through the heaviness of the cheese.

Acidity tends to be more noticeable and more prone to pairings in white wines. Although red wines have acids in them, acids in red wines take a back seat to tannins, alcohol, and body in red wine pairings.

Understanding Sweetness in Pairings

Just as acidity makes up part of the intensity equation, so does sweetness and, like acidity, it also needs to be considered by itself in pairings.

Sweet Wines with Sweet Foods

Sweet wines tend to love sweet foods. The general rule for pairing by sweetness is to make sure that the wine is always sweeter than the food.

This is a pretty easy rule to follow when pairing savory dishes or most appetizers, entrées, soups, and salads because they are rarely sweet. But this can definitely become an issue when you are pairing desserts. Desserts must be paired with wines that taste sweeter. If your wine is less sweet than your dessert, when they are served together, the wine might taste sour or bitter.

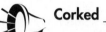 **Corked**

The sweetness rule needs to be considered on those rare occasions when you are serving a sweet entrée. Fruit dumplings, fruit soups, and fruit salads all should be paired with wines that are much sweeter than they are.

Sweet Wines with Salty and Spicy Foods

You also need to take a wine's sweetness into account when pairing with salty and spicy foods. This is a case of opposites attracting. The sweetness of a wine will balance out the saltiness of a food. Salty pretzels taste great with sweet wines. To understand this, think of a caramel-chocolate truffle. Very often, just a touch of sea salt sprinkled on the top, brightens the whole chocolate.

Salt brings out a food's sweet qualities because our sweet and our salt sensors on our taste buds overlap on our tongues. When tasted together, they bring out a second level of flavors.

Sweet wines can also be used to balance spicy food. Indian, Chinese, Thai, and Mexican dishes that have a lot of heat need to be balanced with a sweeter wine. A spicy wasabi-covered piece of sashimi should be paired up with a sweet Riesling. Sweet barbecue ribs can be paired up with a Shiraz with a higher alcohol content, but the minute you turn up the heat in the barbecue sauce, you're going to need to look for another wine, perhaps a fruity, somewhat sweet Zinfandel.

Pairing Concepts: Intensity, Acid, and Sweetness

The following cheat sheet offers some examples of how to go about pairing by intensity, acid, and sweetness.

Acid Likes Acid

Dish: Chicken piccata
Wine: Chablis or other high-acid Chardonnay

Dish: Tomato soup
Wine: Sangiovese

Dish: Goat cheese tart
Wine: Sauvignon Blanc

Acid Cuts Fat

Dish: Cheesy polenta
Wine: Pinot Grigio

Dish: Lobster with drawn butter
Wine: Unoaked Chardonnay

Dish: Beef stroganoff
Wine: Barbera, Rhone reds

Sweet Likes Sweet

Dish: Chocolate chip cookies
Wine: Madeira

Dish: Sweet potatoes with marshmallows
Wine: PX Sherry

Dish: Glazed ham
Wine: Beaujolais, Gewürztraminer

Sweet Likes Salty

Dish: Potato chips
Wine: Demi-sec or sweeter Champagne, Moscato d'Asti

Dish: Beef teriyaki
Wine: Beaujolais

Dish: Ham
Wine: Beaujolais, Gewürztraminer

Intensity Likes Intensity

Dish: Meatloaf
Wine: Cabernet Sauvignon, Merlot

Dish: Barbeque chicken
Wine: Zinfandel

Dish: Beef stew
Wine: Malbec, Merlot, Cabernet Sauvignon

Spicy Likes Sweet

Dish: Spicy tuna hand roll
Wine: Off-dry Riesling

Dish: Jalapeño poppers
Wine: Sweet Riesling or Pinot Gris

Dish: Buffalo wings
Wine: Sweet Riesling, Moscato d'Asti

The Least You Need to Know

♦ In general, like pairs with like. That means intensity loves intensity, acid loves acid, and sweetness loves sweetness.

♦ Spicy foods should be paired with sweeter wines that are less intense.

♦ Acidity can cut through rich dishes.

♦ To improve the pairing of an acidic wine with a dish, squeeze a lemon or lime over the dish.

♦ Always pair sweeter wines with sweet foods.

♦ Sweet wines love spicy and salty dishes.

Chapter 12

The Artistry of Pairing: Using Your Intuition

In This Chapter

- ◆ Understanding the artistry of pairings
- ◆ Using your intuition to pair wines with foods
- ◆ How other pairing principles come into play
- ◆ The role of aromas in intuitive pairings

Pairing wine with food is often described as an art, and this chapter explores the artistry that can be involved when pairing wine with food.

Another way to describe the artistry of pairings is to call it "intuitive pairing," meaning that your likes and dislikes come into play.

How you identify and explore the aromas of wines also comes into the intuitive pairing process. What you enjoy—whether taste or smell—comes out in your final pairings. Learning more about aromas will help you expand your pairing repertoire.

Using Your Intuition

If pairing by science uses measurable, quantifiable characteristics, pairing by artistry uses less exact means. The artistry or intuition of pairing is accomplished not by weighing or calculating specific factors but by using your personal background, tastes, and experience with wine and food to devise a suitable match.

When you use your intuition to solve a problem, you bring past knowledge, information, and experience to bear on a current situation. For example, you know your wife loves roses, and she adores her new car. Therefore, she'll probably appreciate the rose-scented car freshener you picked up for her. Or you know your nephew was captivated by the dragons in the *Harry Potter* series, so he'll be equally excited when he learns that you're taking him to see that new dragon movie. Or you know you love raspberries, and you also like balsamic vinegar so you'll probably enjoy the chef's special, which combines raspberries and a balsamic reduction over a wild rice pilaf.

> **Wine Nerd**
>
> There's a Cabernet Sauvignon blend made by Bergevin Lane Vineyards in Washington that is called Intuition Reserve. According to one reviewer, it has dark cherry notes with a hint of tobacco and would pair well with lasagna or chicken parmagiana.

Using your intuition with wine pairing can be as simple as knowing that a really heavy Cabernet Sauvignon will not work well with a delicate ceviche. It's sometimes just knowing the obvious—like that adding a cup of salt to a cheesecake recipe isn't going to work. The way you recognize the obvious is to become more educated about a subject, and the best way to do that is to experience it.

With wine and food matching that sometimes means you're going to taste wines you don't like, and sometimes you're going to taste wines and foods together that you don't like. But through the process of tasting you're also going to discover what you do like and what you absolutely love, and you're going to be able to apply your likes and dislikes to future pairings.

To get better at pairing by artistry, first, determine what you do like with wines and wine and food pairings. You probably already have a baseline of your likes and dislikes when it comes to taste, but when you think of your next pairing, it wouldn't hurt to jot down your likes and dislikes.

Wine Nerd

Though we both feel we have a pretty good sense of what we like and dislike, we also know it helps to keep a record of our tastes in a wine and food journal. We encourage you to do the same. You can use any old journal or notebook to do this, but Appendix B is a tasting journal template that you can copy or use as a starting point.

Other Pairings: Principles and Intuition

Intuition is sometimes described as "knowing what you know, but not knowing exactly why you know it." Some pairing principles fall under this description, including "red goes with red, white goes with white" and "goes with where it grows" or pairing by terroir.

Both of these principles also can be described as obvious, or easy, pairing principles. But the main reason why they fall into the artistic or intuitive category is that, even though we can describe them and their history, we don't know exactly how they work.

Additionally, these two principles aren't very measurable. You're not measuring the redness of the wine up against the redness of the meat. And you're not measuring how French a wine is against how French a dish is. In both cases, you know what you know, and you know that they work.

The Art of Aromas

When we first started tasting wine and heard other people describe a wine as having aromas of citrus or berries or tobacco, we would nod our heads in agreement, but we were really just thinking, "hey, this smells like, well, wine." But the more we tasted wine, the more we understood the importance of using our experiences with the aromas of food and other substances to discern those same qualities in wine.

If you have never tasted a gooseberry, you aren't going to be able to use that as an aromatic descriptor for Sauvignon Blanc. If you've never smelled a lychee, you won't be able to say Gewürztraminer smells like one. Experiencing a wide variety of fruits, vegetables, soils, flowers, trees—and basically anything else you can get your nose into—will help you better describe what you smell in wine.

Smell is a powerful sense and can call to mind long-lost memories. For instance, a wine with aromas of pencil lead and wood shavings can recall childhood memories of elementary school—even particular grades, classes, and teachers.

> **Wine Nerd**
>
> Noted wine reviewer Robert Parker's website includes the "Asian Food Lexicon for Wine," which lists more than 40 different Asian foods and ingredients matched with wines that contain similar textures or aromatics. Go to www.erobertparker.com and click on "in Asia," then "Asian Food Lexicon."

> **Perfect Pairings**
>
> Dark chocolate and red wine, especially Zinfandels, are an intuitive pairing, and they nearly always work, one elevating the other to new taste levels.

While most wine connoisseurs can identify different aromas in different wines, not everyone will agree on which aromas can be found in which wines. One person might smell apple aromas while another might detect pear notes. Unlike acidity, sweetness, and alcohol content—which all have definite, measurable characteristics—aromas are more subjective.

Aromas are definitely personal. No two noses—on wine or on people—are alike. You can't definitively say "This Zinfandel has 90 percent cherry notes and 10 percent cocoa notes." You'll more likely say "This reminds me of a chocolate-covered cherry."

One example of an aromatic, intuitive pairing is to take a smoky, bacon-scented Rhone and pair it with a bacon-laden dish. You can also take a mushroom or truffle-scented Nebbiolo and match it with a mushroom risotto.

The Art of Textures

Describing the *texture* of a wine is also more of an art than an exact science. A really silky wine, for example, fills your mouth and coats your taste buds. When it comes to pairing such a silky wine, you need to ask yourself if you like to match the luxurious feeling or balance it out.

def•i•ni•tion

Texture describes the mouth-feel of a wine.

Like aromas, you can't measure a texture. You can only describe it. One person's silky wine is another person's oily wine. It really depends on personal preferences and experiences. Tannin, viscosity, effervescence, and acidity will all affect the mouthfeel of a wine, but it still remains something that is descriptive rather than quantifiable.

Pairing by Aromas and Textures

When pairing both aromas and textures it's not simply a matter of matching or balancing. You need to look to your own personal tastes. How do you want to play up a wine or a dish? A lot of pairing by texture has to do with what you're after for a particular meal. For instance, you might pair a lobster bisque with an equally creamy Chardonnay to bring out the creaminess in both the food and the wine, or you might choose to cut the fat in the bisque with a crisp Chenin Blanc. Both work, but it just comes down to your personal preference.

Pairing by aromas or textures isn't an exact way to pair. Some Chardonnays will work better with certain lobster bisques, for instance, but some may not work at all. A lobster bisque topped with a lot of different herbs might be better matched with an herbaceous Sauvignon Blanc, for example.

> **Wine Nerd**
>
> After you experience a really good or a really bad pairing, take note of it and figure out what went right or wrong so that you can duplicate or avoid it in the future.

When you are at a pairings dinner, or having your meal paired by a sommelier, be open to trying wines and foods that you might not normally choose. If you are open to having white wine when you usually drink red, you can open the door to a whole new tasting experience. You never know, you might discover a new favorite. Or, you might reinforce your current tastes. In any case, you'll learn something!

As always, taste, taste, and taste some more. The more you taste, the greater your knowledge base will be for the next time you want to pair wine with food.

Artistic Pairing Suggestions

Here are some of our favorite pairings by intuition.

- **80% Dark Chocolate** A Cabernet Sauvignon with strong cocoa aromas, which will parallel those of the chocolate and have a similar tannin structure.

- **Bacon-Wrapped Meatloaf** Southern Rhone Syrah, with smoky, bacon fat aromas, will amplify the bacon flavors while also intuitively matching the intensity.

- **Eggs Benedict** Champagne, the typical brunch beverage, which also intuitively works as contrast to the heavy hollandaise sauce.

- **Egg Foo Young** Australian Shiraz with white pepper aromas that match the white pepper spice in the dish, while intuitively matching the intensity.

- **Seafood Bisque** Oloroso Sherry that has a rich salt-brine flavor and aromas of the sea. Intuitively, the Sherry adds richness and complexity to the meal and is even delicious when added to the soup itself. Some chefs even serve such bisque with a shot of Sherry to drizzle on the soup before eating.

- **Waldorf Salad** Prosecco with strong apple aromas that match the ingredients, is as refreshing as the salad and cuts through the yogurt- or mayonnaise-based dressing.

The Least You Need to Know

◆ Use your personal tastes to come up with pairings.

◆ Keep track of your wine and pairing preferences in a journal to improve your pairing abilities.

◆ "Red goes with red, white goes with white," and "goes with where it grows" are intuitive pairing principles because they are not concretely measurable.

◆ Pairing by aromas and textures is more art than science.

◆ Be open to new pairing suggestions to improve your artistic ability in pairing wines and foods.

Chapter 13

Matching Wine with International Cuisines

In This Chapter

- Matching exotic spices
- Using traditional beverages as a guide
- Pairing Mexican and Caribbean cuisines
- Pairing Asian cuisines
- Pairing European cuisines
- Pairing African and Middle Eastern cuisines

Just a scant 15 or 20 years ago wine snobs scoffed at pairing many "ethnic" cuisines with wine. By ethnic, we mean cuisines from countries such as Mexico and Japan that traditionally have not had corresponding wine regions. Now most restaurants serving international cuisines have decent wine lists, and many gourmet chefs incorporate international spices and dishes into their menus.

This chapter dives right into the logistics of pairing international cuisines with wines. You'll find out how to match "exotic" spices or flavors with more commonplace spices and flavors, and learn to use traditional beverages as a guide to picking out wines.

Problems Posed by International Cuisines

The basic pairings principles, excluding the "goes with where it grows" rule, can all be applied to international cuisines, or cuisines where grapes have not traditionally been cultivated. But simply knowing that you can match flavors with aromas or intensity with intensity might not always help you when it comes to finding the perfect wines to match with an international meal.

Sometimes, it's hard enough matching a familiar flavor with an aroma. When you begin to enter the realm of more exotic, or less common, flavors and spices, it can get tricky.

Finding a Common Ground

But keep in mind that most international dishes often have something in common with more traditional cuisines. Mexican and Chinese dishes often incorporate cinnamon, for example. Thai and Vietnamese cuisines often have a bit of French flair to them. And fish and chips—an English pub staple—isn't that different from American bar food.

As with any dish, you should first break it down into its various components or flavors. If you can identify some common ingredients, tastes, or textures then use that as a jumping off point for your pairing. A Thai noodle dish that contains a lot of lemongrass, for example, would likely pair well with wines that usually pair well with lemony dishes. A crisp Pinot Gris would likely work in this instance.

Spicy Matches

As with any pairing, break down an exotic sauce or dish into its components. Next, determine if any of the key ingredients or spices are similar to foods you are more readily able to pair. Many unusual spices, herbs and other ingredients have a conventional parallel you can use to help in the pairing.

Here's a quick list of parallel flavors:

Cilantro, while distinctive in its taste, can be paired similarly to basil and mint.

Cardamom has a similar sweetness to cinnamon or cloves.

Lemongrass is like an herbal lemon.

Cumin has an earthy, almost mushroomy aroma.

Chinese five-spice powder contains cinnamon and pepper, among other ingredients.

Wasabi isn't that different from regular horseradish.

Sweet and sour sauces are sweet with citrusy undertones.

Curry powders have sweet and hot notes, and contain chilies, tumeric, and cumin.

Garam masala contains chilies, peppers, cumin, and cinnamon and like curry powders, has a balance of sweet and hot flavors.

Tamarind is both sweet and tart, similar to citrus fruits.

Soy sauce is salty and contains strong umami flavors.

Teriyaki is salty, sweet, and a bit earthy in flavor.

Chickpeas are similar to white beans.

Mole sauces contain chocolate and chilies.

Salsas often have cilantro, chilies, and tomatoes.

Spicy International Dishes

Chili pepper is a very common ingredient in many international cuisines. And even though there are dozens of different kinds of chilies—and they can be dried, fresh, or powdered—they all add heat to a dish.

The hotter the chili pepper, the hotter the dish. And when it comes to heat, think intensity. You already know that you shouldn't match that heavy heat with a heavy or high-alcohol wine. Instead, match it with a wine that is as intensely sweet as the dish is intensely hot.

Whenever you're dealing with a spicy dish, the main rule is to pair it with a sweet or off-dry wine. Forget tannins, and forget trying to match anything else with the dish. If it's spicy, you must go sweet. It doesn't matter if the dish is primarily composed of beef, and you think beef is best with Cabernet. It doesn't matter if the dish is creamy and rich like a Chardonnay, or that it contains mushrooms that might pair with a Pinot Noir.

You don't want to ignore the dish's other characteristics or flavors altogether, however. After you've determined you need a sweet wine to offset the heat, then you can pair to the other characteristics of the dish. For instance, if a dish has mushrooms in it, you might opt for a sweet German Spätburgunder. A spicy seafood dish? How about a sweet Riesling?

Just how much heat there is—and how high your heat threshold is—will help you determine where in the range of sweetness, from off-dry to syrupy-sweet, you'll need to go. The spicier the dish, the sweeter the wine you will need to pair.

> **Perfect Pairings**
>
> Many international cuisines have some sort of fried appetizer, such as samosas, egg rolls, crab rolls. Fried foods are best paired with a sparkling wine. And if these hors d'oeuvres are served with a sweet and sour dipping sauce, go with a sweeter bubbly.

Pairing by Traditional Beverages

Before people started pairing international cuisines with wine, they usually served them with a traditional beverage. Chinese food? Black tea. Japanese cuisine? Green tea and sake. English stew? An ale, of course.

Instead of pairing by "goes with where it grows," an obvious parallel is to "go with what usually is drunk." The idea is to take that traditional beverage and see if you can find a wine that is similar to it.

Scandinavian cuisine, for example, is often served with aquavit, and Polish dishes are often served with vodka. A parallel wine would be an aromatically potent white like Viognier or even a dry White Port.

Green teas are similar to Sauvignon Blanc and Pinot Gris—they're herbaceous and light.

Thai iced coffees and iced teas are sweet and creamy—a Chenin Blanc, perhaps?

Stout beer and whiskies, served alongside Irish stew, could be replaced with a rich and woody Cabernet.

Wine Nerd

Not all beers or teas are created equal. In general, lighter beers equal lighter wines, and lighter teas equal lighter wines. For more ideas about beer and tea parallels, check out Chapter 17, which discusses food pairings with other beverages.

Pairing Mexican and Caribbean Cuisines

With both Mexican and Caribbean foods, the defining characteristic is heat. Jalapeños, habaneros, and banana peppers all have heat. While their heat levels on the *Scoville scale* varies, you have to pair them with a wine that will soothe your taste buds.

def•i•ni•tion

The **Scoville scale** measures the amount of heat in a pepper in Scoville heat units, or SHU. The heat comes from the amount of a chemical compound called capsaicin in the pepper. The scale ranges from 0 SHU (sweet bell peppers) to 325,000 SHU (habañero peppers) to 5.3 million SHU (police grade pepper spray) to 16 million SHU (pure capsaicin).

You already know that if a dish is spicy, that is the first and foremost characteristic to pair it by. Sweet Rieslings, Gewürztraminers, and even Lambruscos can be paired with Mexican foods because they are sweet, and sweet tames the heat.

But not all Mexican or Caribbean dishes are that hot. Some are pretty mild.

Wine Nerd

If the seeds and the core of a pepper are removed before they are added to a dish, it won't be as hot. The seeds and the core are what contain the capsaicin in the pepper. Guacamole, for example, often contains seeded and cored jalapeños and so isn't very hot at all.

Very often, Mexican cuisine incorporates moles or complex sauces that often contain chocolate, nuts, and seeds that are ground down and cooked for hours. If the moles aren't too hot, you can pair them with a heavy Zinfandel or Syrah, which will mimic the cocoa and nutty flavors in the mole sauce. But if they are hot, go for a sweet red like Lambrusco or Brachetto.

Salsas often contain tomatoes or tomatillos. If they're hot, go sweet. If they are mild and green, you can go with a white wine like Albariño; if the salsa is pink like some pico de gallo salsas, you can also go with a white or rosé wine; if the salsa is red, go with a red wine like Sangiovese or Tempranillo. Albariños have a crispness that matches that of tomatillos, and Sangioveses and Tempranillos have tomato notes and complementary acidity.

Avocados and beans—mainly pinto, red, and black—are also used frequently in Mexican cooking. Avocados tend to pair well with Chardonnay and Grüner Veltliner, and beans, especially refried beans, pair well with Rhone reds. Both ingredients, being rich and creamy, are also delicious with sparkling wines.

Wine Nerd

Wine grapes traditionally haven't been cultivated in Mexico, but the country has a few burgeoning wine regions and is beginning to export some wines. It's not a force in the wine world currently, but expect that to change within the next decade or so.

Spicy Caribbean cuisine, like Jamaican jerk chicken, can be paired with off-dry Riesling or Syrah. But very often these dishes contain tropical sauces and fruits that would pair better with wines containing tropical aromas, Sauvignon Blanc, Chardonnay, and Gewürztraminer are often a good match. Plantains, a bananalike ingredient that's common in Caribbean fare, can be paired with wines that have a banana aroma, like Beaujolais Nouveau or Chardonnay.

Caribbean and Mexican dishes often incorporate a lot of vegetables. If the vegetables take a starring role, reach for a Sauvignon Blanc.

Pairing Asian Cuisines

Many Asian cuisines incorporate plain white or Jasmine rice. A really good match for rice by itself is Chardonnay.

Asian cuisines can often be tricky to match. If the dish is spicy-hot, as is the case with many Szechwan dishes, head to the sweet wines. With sweet and sour dishes, you have two choices: play up the sweetness or match with the sour.

As with any dish, analyze it and break it down into its components. Moo-shu pork, for example, contains pork, a thin pancake, mushrooms, and vegetables, but the overriding flavor comes from its plum sauce. Plum aromas can often be found in a Dolcetto, and so it would be a good match for this dish.

While Chinese cuisine often layers flavor upon flavor, Japanese cuisine tends to focus on a single, often delicate, flavor. For example, sushi is quite delicate, as are the appetizers, such as steamed dumplings and seaweed salad, that often are served before it. Sushi is traditionally served with sake, a drink made of fermented rice. Sauvignon Blanc, Pinot Gris, and Riesling have some similar body and acid characteristics as sake and go very well with sushi.

Not all Japanese dishes are delicate. Teriyaki and tonkatsu (fried meat, especially pork) dishes are heavy, and they pair well with lighter reds and sparkling wines. Tempura, as with other fried foods, goes really well with sparkling wines.

Indian cuisine is quite complex, very aromatic, and often spicy. You already know to pair any hot dishes with sweet wines; noted Indian cookbook author, Monica Bhide often pairs Gewürztraminer or German Rieslings with her dishes.

Wine Nerd
Japan has a small wine industry on the far northern island of Hokkaido. Some of these wines pair well with Japanese foods but, unfortunately, they aren't exported to the United States.

Not all Indian food is spicy. Samosas and other fried appetizers go great with sparkling wines, as the bubbles cut some of the grease. Rich, creamier dishes like saag paneer (spinach with paneer cheese) go well with buttery Chardonnays if you're pairing to match, but they also work well with Pinot Gris if you're looking to counterbalance the richness.

Wine Nerd

India does make some wines, and we've seen a few make their way to Indian restaurants in the United States. Try the sweeter white wines from India if you get a chance, as they pair perfectly with Indian cuisine. India cultivates both white and red grapes, including Chenin Blanc, Sauvignon Blanc, Cabernet Sauvignon, and Shiraz.

Corked

Some wines contain trace amounts of animal products such as egg and gelatin, which are used to clarify the wine in a process called fining. If you are a vegan and you want to avoid these wines, you'll either have to inquire at the winery or the wine store or look for a wine label that states that the wine is "un-fined."

Vietnamese and Thai foods, like Indian cuisine, are quite aromatic, but with quite different aromas. Cilantro, lemongrass, and ginger often make their way into Thai and Vietnamese dishes.

Chile peppers also are common in Vietnamese and Thai cuisines, and Thai peppers, especially, are quite hot. Once again—last time, we promise!—if a dish has chile peppers in any amount, go with a sweet wine. If it is a fried dish, sparkling wine works well.

If the overriding flavor is lemongrass, try an herbaceous Sauvignon Blanc. If the overriding flavor is ginger, go with a Gewürztraminer or Viognier.

Another thing to note, especially with Vietnamese dishes, is that there are some parallels to French cuisine. If the dish isn't too hot, look to those parallels and see if it matches up with French dishes. Vietnamese sandwiches, for example, are made with French bread, and some even contain paté. As such, pair with a French Pinot Noir.

Pairing "Other" European Cuisines

While grapes grow in many areas of Europe, the entire continent isn't covered with vineyards. The British Isles aren't known for their wines; neither are the Scandinavian countries of Sweden, Finland, and Norway; and neither are Poland and Russia.

English and Irish cuisines often are typically quite heavy—they are meat-based and hearty. Pair up rich stews with Merlot or Cabernet, bangers and mash with Côtes du Rhônes, and you can't go wrong with serving fish and chips with Champagne.

Some Irish dishes contain a lot of herbs like thyme or rosemary. In these cases look for wines that have herbal aromas like Grüner Veltliner, Sauvignon Blanc, or Sangiovese.

Polish, Russian, and even Czech cuisines are so similar to German cuisine that you can pretty much follow the German "goes with where it grows" rule, but breaking down the dishes into their primary ingredients can help you pair with other varietals, too. For example, Russian borscht, made up primarily of beets and vegetables, tastes great with Sangiovese or Carignan.

Scandinavian dishes incorporate a lot of fish, so white wines, in general, work well. For dishes that are topped with lingonberry jam, try an equally fruity and tangy Pinot Noir from New Zealand or Oregon.

Pairing African and Middle Eastern Cuisines

Like Indian cuisine, African cuisine can be quite aromatic, but it is typically not quite as hot.

North African cuisine, in particular, has much in common with Mediterranean cuisine, using tomatoes, olives, lemons, and nuts, it also often incorporates lamb, chicken, and spices such as saffron, ginger, and cinnamon. One-pot dishes, like Moroccan tagines, make heavy use of vegetables. This cuisine often works well with Albariños and medium-bodied, Spanish reds.

It also should be noted that some South African wineries have made efforts to pair South African dishes with their wines. The South African wine industry is still growing and, like Australian and American wineries, you can't always rely on the "goes with where it grows" rule because South African wineries are quite experimental.

> **Perfect Pairings**
>
> Moroccan and Northern African cuisines can be described as Moorish, and the Moors, before they were kicked out of Spain, left quite an imprint on Spanish cuisine. For this reason, milder, fruity reds and whites from Spain tend to work well with African cuisine.

Ethiopian cuisine has some parallels with Indian and Moroccan cuisines, and it often uses a lot of vegetables and a bit of spice. Rieslings work well, and fruitier, low-alcohol reds also do quite nicely. Beaujolais and Pinot Noir are delicious with kitfo, an Ethiopian steak tartare.

Middle Eastern cuisine has a lot of similarities with Mediterranean cuisine—the olives; the fresh, briny cheeses; the phyllo dough; the lamb; and so on. And grapes have been grown in the Middle East for years and years. But for the purposes of pairings, you're really not going to have an easy time finding imported Middle Eastern wines. So while you could do "goes with where it grows," you probably won't be able to find any of the wines made there to match the dishes.

Instead, look to Spanish, Greek, and Italian wines, especially those used to pair with seafood and coastal dishes. Albariños, Txakolis, and Pinot Grigios are a good choice. And if the dish contains olive or lamb, it is likely those flavors will be the overriding taste of the dish. Look to wines that have matching aromas like Sherries, dry rosés, and Tempranillos.

Suggested International Pairings

Here is a sampling of international dishes and the wines that match them:

Adobo pork (Mexican)   Petite Sirah, Shiraz, Zinfandel

Baba ghannouj (Middle Eastern)   Pinot Grigio, dry rosé, sparkling wine

Baklava (Middle Eastern)   Muscat, Tawny Port, Tokaji

Bangers and mash (English)   Red Rhone blends, Tempranillo, sparkling rosé

Bánh mì (Vietnamese)   Pinot Blanc, sparkling wines, dry rosé

Beef sukiyaki (Japanese)   Australian Shiraz

Borscht (Russian)   Sangiovese, Carignan

Callaloo (Caribbean)   Pinot Gris/Grigio, South African Chardonnay

Caviar and blinis (Russian)   Sparkling wine, especially Champagne

Chicken satay (Singaporean)   Off-dry Riesling, Sémillon, Pinot Noir

Doro wat (Ethiopian)   Off-dry Chenin Blanc, Riesling

Falafel (Middle Eastern)   Sauvignon Blanc, Albariño, sparkling wine

Fish and chips (English)   Sparkling wine

Guacamole (Mexican)   Grüner Veltliner, Torrontés, Sauvignon Blanc, Chardonnay

Hummus (Middle Eastern)   Pinot Gris/Grigio, dry rosé

Jamaican jerk chicken (Caribbean)   Off-dry Riesling, Gewürztraminer

Kimchi (Korean)   Off-dry to sweet Riesling, Beaujolais

Kitfo (Ethiopian)   Beaujolais, Pinot Noir

Kroppkaka (Scandinavian)   Pinot Noir, especially from Oregon or New Zealand

Lamb tagine (Moroccan)   Tempranillo, Syrah, especially Spanish

Lingonberry jam (Scandinavian)   Pinot Noir, especially from Oregon or New Zealand

Mofongo (Caribbean)   Beaujolais

Mole (Mexican)   Zinfandel, Shiraz, Lambrusco, Brachetto

Moo-shu pork (Chinese)   Dolcetto, medium-bodied Merlot

Murgh Makhani (Indian)   Off-dry Pinot Blanc, Riesling

Pad Thai (Thai) Off-dry Gewürztraminer or Chenin Blanc

Peking duck (Chinese) Pinot Noir, off-dry Riesling

Phó (Vietnamese) Pinot Noir, especially South American

Pickled herring (Scandinavian) Fino Sherry, Viognier

Pierogi (Polish) Dry Riesling, Chardonnay

Saag paneer (Indian) Chardonnay, Pinot Gris/Grigio

Samosas (Indian) Sparkling wine

Swedish meatballs (Scandinavian) Pinot Noir, especially New Zealand

Tandoori chicken (Indian) Chardonnay, Beaujolais

Teriyaki chicken (Japanese) Off-dry to sweet Riesling, Gewürztraminer, Pinot Noir

Tonkatsu (Japanese) Sparkling wine, especially rosés

Tostones (Caribbean) Chardonnay, sparkling wines

Vegetable egg rolls (Chinese) Sparkling wine, Grüner Veltliner

Yaki udon (Japanese) Grüner Veltliner, Chardonnay, sparkling wine

The Least You Need to Know

- If the dish is the least bit hot, tame the heat with a sweet wine.

- Try to match flavors with aromas in international dishes.

- For less familiar flavors, try to identify a similar, more traditional flavor and match to that (like lemongrass for lemon).

- Find a parallel beverage that is served with the cuisine, and seek to find a wine that mimics its characteristics.

Chapter **14**

Experimental Pairings

In This Chapter

- ◆ The benefit of experimenting with pairings
- ◆ Experimentation basics
- ◆ Setting up your own pairing experiments
- ◆ Pairing wine with music and art

Chefs, vintners, and oenophiles everywhere seek to find the next big pairing. This experimentation has led to some crazy matches, but it has also led to some pretty darn good pairings, too.

This chapter encourages you to combine your inner wine geek with your inner mad scientist. You'll find out how to use your palate as the starting point and move on from there.

Though it sometimes seems like a chef is working magic when he dazzles you with an unusual pairing, such as sparkling Shiraz with chicken, we'll reveal some of his secrets to you. Like a magician showing you where the rabbit went after he stuffed it into his hat, this chapter will show you how the food and wine experts experiment to come up with some wild pairings.

Besides revealing the basics of pairing experimentation, you'll find out how to set up your own experiments with wine and food and learn about some "other" experimental pairings with wine—including music and art. Finally, you'll find a list of some experimental pairings for you to try at home.

It All Begins with Your Tastes

Before you can really even begin to experiment with pairings, you need to understand your own personal preferences—your likes and dislikes. That's because the starting point for experimentation is your tastes and preferences. If you love Chardonnay, then that's where you should start. If you're a fan of big reds, then begin there.

To better understand what you like, you first need to ask yourself some questions:

♦ What wines do you like?

♦ What wine and food pairings have enchanted you?

♦ What flavors and aromas excite you?

Knowing what you like is important in pairing because you're more apt to end up liking experiments that involve the flavors, textures, and aromas that you enjoy. If you're not a big fan of red wines with a lot of tannins, then you're probably not going to like pairings that play off of those tannins.

That's why it's important to keep track of what wines you like and what pairings you enjoy. You can do this by simply jotting things down in a journal; keeping a small, spiral bound notebook in your purse; or keeping a record on your BlackBerry or iPhone. If you're not sure where to start, check out Appendix B, which is a template for a wine journal.

Be sure to note *why* you liked a particular wine or pairing. What is it, specifically, about the wine or the pairing that stands out to you? Do you like Italian wines because of their terroir aromatics? Their weight? The way they remind you of your favorite vacation?

Once you know the why, then you can apply the specifics to other wines or other pairings. For example, let's say you just loved a

Chardonnay with your clam chowder. What about that Chardonnay did you like with that pairing? Let's say you've narrowed it down to the buttery, oaky aromas. Once you know that, the next time you have clam chowder, you can try an oak-fermented Chenin Blanc. That is how you start experimenting.

Figuring out the "why" of your likes and dislikes is not only good for your own experimentations, but it also is good for introducing friends and loved ones to new wines. For example, Jeanette's husband adores big Cabs. What he really likes is their intensity and tannins, so Jeanette introduced him to Rioja, which he now loves as much as he does Cabernet.

Perfect Pairings

Finding out the why is especially important when trying to introduce White Zinfandel aficionados to other wines. Most likely, people who like White Zinfandel are attracted to its sweetness. So bring out a bottle of sweet Riesling and tell them, "I've found a wine I think you'll like."

Understanding Experimentation

People often tell us about having enjoyed amazing and unusual pairings that a chef and vintner came up with at a restaurant-hosted wine dinner, but then they were unable to replicate the experience at home. How can the chef and vintner come up with such perfect pairings, and why is it so hard to repeat on your own?

The method chefs, sommeliers, and winemakers use to come up with out-of-the-ordinary pairings is actually quite simple. Drawing on their knowledge of flavors and aromas, they seek a match, and then they use one magic tool: their taste buds.

Before a big wine dinner, most chefs and sommeliers do a dry run to see if the pairings they came up with actually work. Jaclyn has helped organize hundreds of such dinners and knows that it's not magic, it's just taste. It's the same way a chef knows if a dish needs more salt—he or she tastes it.

If you're planning a pairing, we recommend you do your own dry run. Unless, of course, you want to be surprised.

Pairing Food to a Particular Wine

When pairing a particular bottle of wine to food, you don't have to do a full dry run, you just need to make the sauce that you are pairing and divide it up into anywhere from three to ten bowls. Then do something a bit different with each bowl of sauce, being sure to record how you've altered each bowl. Add a little more sugar to one, add some different herbs to another, and so on. For example, if you're planning to pair barbecue sauce and ribs to a particular wine, make the barbecue sauce, divide it into several bowls. Add salt to one bowl, add rubs to another, and to others add spices, hot pepper, and so on.

Taste each version of the sauce with the wine you're planning to pair with the dish. Chances are one of these sauces is going to taste better with the wine. That is the version of the sauce that you are going to want to use for the meal.

Pairing Wine to a Particular Food

If you are planning to make a special sauce—let's say, Grandma's spaghetti sauce—you instead want to pair the wine to the sauce. Pick out anywhere from 3 to 12 wines, make up a batch of sauce, and start tasting.

Obviously, this type of pairing technique can make a dent in your budget, but this is actually what many chefs and sommeliers do. If a meal is very special, we do recommend that you test out a few wines. You can even try different varieties of the same varietal. At a wine dinner Jeanette attended at Firefly Restaurant in Wauwatosa, Wisconsin, the sommelier tried 20 different Pinot Noirs from the Willamette Valley with a smoked salmon dish.

After you come up with your perfect pairing—and even if you come up with a not-so-good pairing—keep notes. That's how you will remember what works and doesn't work. In addition to writing down the wine and the dish that you liked, mention *why* you liked it. The specifics of the pairing will help you when you pair up other dishes.

Being Smart about Experimentation

Obviously, you can pair a heavy Cab with a seafood salad or match a light white with a big steak, and once in a while, such odd pairings can work. But instead of trying to force opposite flavors and aromas, it's best to start out trying to match flavors and aromas.

You'll have much better success if you start out with the goal of matching, rather than overcoming, particular flavors or aromas. Let's say you have a great chicken pot pie and in the past you've successfully paired it with a buttery Chardonnay that matches the buttery, flaky crust perfectly. Even though you are satisfied with your standard pairing, you want to try something different.

The first way to go about it is to try to find a wine that's similar to your Chardonnay—an oak-fermented Chenin Blanc might work. Or you could look at other elements in the dish to pair. Instead of the buttery, flaky crust, why not pair to your seasonings? If you used lots of white pepper, thyme, and rosemary, you might try an herbal Grüner Veltliner which, with its high acid levels, can cut through the creamy filling and match the seasonings. If the filling has sweet notes, try a Riesling.

Many times when chefs and sommeliers experiment with pairings, they use sauces and ingredients to create a bridge with the pairings. This technique can be particularly useful if you know a wine works with an entrée, and you're trying to tie that wine to the appetizer, salad, or soup. For example, if you are serving a roast that you know works perfectly with a Cabernet Sauvignon, and you want to serve that wine with the salad, think of what you can do to make the salad more palatable to the wine. Adding some blue cheese, cocoa nibs, or even dried cherries might make it match the red wine better.

You might even come up with an amazing new pairing. Jaclyn did just that when she ordered an entrée of duck and a glass of Côtes du Rhône to accompany it.

Perfect Pairings

Don't forget that whenever you have a sauce in a dish you're experimenting with you can add the wine directly to the sauce to create a more direct bridge tying the wine and the dish together. This is especially useful for experimental pairings.

The simple wedge salad that accompanied the meal was topped with very spicy French dressing, blue cheese crumbles, and herbal croutons. The combination of the dressing, the blue cheese, and those homemade croutons matched up perfectly with the intense red wine!

Another technique for experimentation goes back to our very first point of the chapter—looking at what you like. But instead of saying "I like Cabernet Sauvignons because they're tannic so I'm going to try a heavy Syrah," look at your various culinary likes, too, not just your wine preferences.

If you like pineapple and cottage cheese together, you probably would like a creamy Chardonnay with pineapple aromas. If you like black pepper on your food, you probably would like a Shiraz. That Chardonnay might pair beautifully with pineapple cheesecake, and that Shiraz might be a perfect match for a pepper-encrusted filet mignon.

The idea is to put together similar flavors. That is actually how chefs create new dishes. Say a chef likes a basic pesto sauce, but also loves cilantro. The chef replaces the basil in his pesto recipe with cilantro to come up with cilantro pesto, which perfectly accents some empanadas. You can apply this same technique to wine and food pairings. When you use this technique with wines, match the aromas of the new wines with dishes. For example, if you know a Pinot Noir with mushroom aromas matches a mushroom risotto, then you might also be able to pair that same risotto with a Syrah that has mushroom aromas. It's a different pairing that might bring out even more nuances in the dish.

In addition to coming up with different flavors, you can also use wine to enliven a dish that is lacking something. Let's say you made a steak, but it really needed more pepper. Pour a glass of Shiraz—the pepper notes in the wine will enhance the steak as if you had rubbed it with actual peppercorns. If your seafood could use a squeeze of lemon, pour a glass of unoaked Chardonnay.

"Other" Experimental Pairings with Wine

One of the growing movements in wine pairings is to pair wine with things other than food. The two most popular experimental pairings are to match up wine with music or with art. These pairings draw on the senses beyond taste and smell.

Pairing Wine and Music

Adding the aural component takes the pairing to an entirely new level. This can be especially fun if you are a music lover. Try pairing Italian wines with opera to transport you back to Florence. Match heavy, tannic reds with heavy metal music as both have a bold, in-your-face intensity. Enjoy sparkling wines with whimsical ragtime as both are effervescent and uplifting.

How does this work? Music always enhances a dining experience. When entertaining, music sometimes is the last thing people think of, but it really has an effect on a dinner party. The right tempo and beat can keep a party moving at the pace you desire.

Perfect Pairings

If you're not sure where to begin with wine and music pairings, a good website is www.wineandmusic.com. Run by sommelier Jonathan Mitchell, this site offers suggestions like Sade and 2002 Northstar Merlot, or Michael Bublé and a "young, rich California Chardonnay." The site also features an entire section on entertaining tips.

Pairing Wine and Art

While both wine and food do involve the sense of sight, they're not quite as visual an experience as art.

When pairing wine with artwork, match the color and feel of a piece of art with the color and feel of a wine. Keep in mind that soothing colors match soothing or earthy wines. Blues and earth tones, for example, work well with earthy wines like France's Châteauneuf-du-Pape or Italy's Valpolicella. Vibrant and bright colors go with bright noted wines like Pinot Gris. Pastoral scenes are enhanced by grassy wines like Sauvignon Blanc.

Perfect Pairings

If you have returned from a trip and you're sharing your pictures with your family or friends, pair the wine with the trip photos. If you went to Italy, serve some Italian wine while you're perusing photos of Tuscany.

Another thing to consider with art is the texture of the food and, to a lesser extent, the wine. If you're showcasing some textural, sculptural work, something like a paella, a glass of highly textured and bubbly Cava might work.

You can also pair wine, art, music, and food, or any combinations of the four together. The best rule of thumb for both art and music combinations, however, is "like goes with like." It's a bit harder to do opposites pairings.

> **Perfect Pairings**
>
> The two easiest pairing principles to apply to art and music are: "like goes with like," and "goes with where it grows" (or, in this case, originates).

The other easy pairing rule to apply with these experimental pairings is to pair by terroir—Italian music or art paired with Italian wines. And to experiment even more, try pairing sculptures made from granite or other stone with an aromatically stony wine like Chablis.

Suggested Experimental Pairings

Here is a short list of some experimental pairings that you might like to experiment with:

- The movie *Chocolat* paired with a chocolaty, late harvest Zinfandel and some homemade or gourmet chocolates.

- A party or sale featuring a friend's knitting paired with a highly textured and warming Cabernet Sauvignon.

- Black and white photography paired with a clear, white wine like a young Riesling and a dark, black wine like Malbec from France's Cahors region.

- Add wine to Jell-O or plain gelatin and make a uniquely textured wine experience. Gelatinized wine is great with seafood and is also fun to make with sparkling wines, especially rosé.

- Champagne paired with Pop Rocks. Or even better, garnish your favorite dessert, such as cheesecake, with Pop Rocks and serve it with sparkling wine.

- A slideshow of travel photos from your trip to Europe paired with coordinating wines from each of the countries you visited.

- A very jammy Shiraz paired with a peanut butter sandwich.

- Neo-classical metal music paired with a California blended red wine, since both are combinations of old ideas with new techniques.

- A late harvest Riesling paired with filet mignon, served with a Riesling sauce and spring vegetables.

> **Perfect Pairings**
>
> Try lesser-known varietals like Carignan (high-acid red), Mourvèdre (spicy red), Blauer Portugieser (lighter red), Petit Verdot (intense, dark red), Torrontes (floral white), and Roussanne (creamy white) in place of your typical wine preferences when pairing.

The Least You Need to Know

- When experimenting, always start with what you like and go from there.

- Keep a journal of perfect pairs and failed experiments to help guide future pairings.

- Try to combine diverse likes to come up with new pairings.

- Tasting is the secret to most successful pairing experiments.

- Music and art can also be paired with wine.

Part **4**

Pairing Experiences

Wow. You've covered a lot of ground, and by now you have spent quite a bit of time with wine and food. But you're not quite finished yet. The next three chapters will complete your wine and food pairing experience. In them, you will learn about restaurant wine pairing, shopping for wine, throwing a pairing party, and applying wine-pairing principles to other beverages, such as beer, spirits, and coffee.

Chapter 15

Going Out: Restaurant Wine Pairing

In This Chapter

- ◆ Deciphering wine menus
- ◆ Ordering by the glass
- ◆ Understanding sommelier etiquette and bottle service
- ◆ Trying the chef's menu
- ◆ What to do when bad wine comes to your table

One of the best ways to experiment more with wine and food pairings is to enjoy wine service at restaurants. Typically, restaurants carry more bottles than your wine cellar contains, and they often bring in new wines, which are fun to try.

But instead of just randomly ordering off of the menu, there are more satisfying ways to choose your wine at restaurants. This chapter is all about ordering wine at restaurants, and it begins with helping you decipher wine menus. You will learn tips to pick out the best wines for the dishes you're ordering, and find out how to get the most out of a restaurant wine experience.

You will also learn about ordering wine by the glass, sommelier etiquette, chef's menus, and seasonal tasting menus. Finally, we tell you what to do if you're served a bottle of bad wine.

Ordering Wine at a Restaurant

It used to be that when dining at all but the most sophisticated restaurants you had the choice of two, maybe three wines—red or white, and maybe a blush. In the past 10 to 15 years, restaurants have expanded their wine selections to the point where even at the smallest of cafés and bistros there is a plethora of offerings.

Even though most restaurants today serve wine, not every restaurant does it well. And even if a restaurant carries a decent wine list, there's no guarantee that your server will know the difference between Cabernet Sauvignon and Pinot Noir.

If a restaurant is known for having a good wine menu, or if it has a certified sommelier on staff, chances are you'll be in good hands. Traditionally only high-end restaurants and wine bars actually have such a well-trained person on their staff. Some casual restaurants, however, are now recognizing the growing interest in wine and are better training their employees, but this varies from restaurant to restaurant.

Usually the first question out of a server's mouth after you sit down is, "Can I get you something to drink?" If you're not planning to order a predinner cocktail, politely tell the server that you need a few minutes to peruse the wine menu.

Typically, when you order wine at a restaurant, you have a number of decisions to make right off the bat:

Perfect Pairings

Unless there's a wine on the list that you're dying to try, pair the wine to the food. Once you've decided on an entrée, pick a wine that matches it.

- **Do you plan to pair to the food or to the wine?** If you are planning to pair to the food, you need to decide what food you are going to order, and then begin perusing the wine menu. If you are pairing to the wine, look to the wine menu first, moving on to the food menu only after you've made your wine selection.

- **Do you plan to pair a single wine to a single course?** Or will you order a different wine for each course? If you're ordering for a single course, you will most likely pair to the entrée.

- **Do you want to order by the glass or by the bottle?** If the restaurant serves a high volume of wine, it might be better to order by the glass. But if it is a beer place and they don't seem to serve a lot of wine, go with a bottle.

- **How much do you want to spend?** A glass of wine can cost between $4 to $20 or more, depending on the quality of selection. Typically, we recommend spending between $5 to $10 per glass. Bottles of wine at restaurants cost from $15 to thousands. Don't feel pressured to overspend.

 **Corked**

If a restaurant isn't known for its wine, it might not go through bottles very quickly, meaning that you could end up with a glass of wine from a bottle that's been open for several days and is oxidized.

Deciphering the Wine Menu

Wine menus can be set up in as many ways as you might decorate your living room. Some are organized by varietal, region, or from lightest to heaviest. It's all a matter of the designer's personal preference. Sometimes whites are just lumped together, and reds are just lumped together with no apparent order. While it would be nice if all restaurants organized their wines by varietal or from lightest to heaviest—which would make ordering easier—this isn't always the case.

Some wine menus contain brief descriptions of wines, and that's a good starting place. If the menu includes descriptions of the wines, try to match intensity and aromas with the weight and flavors of the food you will be ordering. "A crisp wine with aromas of pear" might be just right for that salad with poached pears. A wine with cherry notes might be suited to that pork tenderloin entrée that has you salivating.

But a lot of times, the wine list is just that—a list of wines, either by the glass or bottle. The list might only give the name of the wine, the maker, the year, and the country of origin.

If that's the kind of list you're presented with, you're going to need to do a little investigating to get a wine that goes with your meal or your course.

Once you've decided on your dish or dishes, look at the menu and try to whittle down your choices. If you ordered tilapia stuffed with crab and served with a beurre blanc sauce, you know that both the fish and the crab are somewhat sweet, so you might decide to go with an off-dry Riesling. But there might be several Rieslings on the menu, none of which you recognize.

Here's where you'll want to ask the server questions:

Is this wine dry or sweet?

Is it fruity or earthy?

Do you think this wine will pair well with this dish?

Which one of these two wines will pair better with this dish?

A knowledgeable waiter or sommelier will not only know the wine list, but he or she will also know what is typically ordered or goes well with the menu items.

While a server might be totally up on the food menu, he or she may be clueless about the wine menu. If you get the sense that you're dealing with a server who knows little about wine, feel free to politely inquire if there is someone else on staff who is more knowledgeable about the wine list.

It never hurts to ask politely for what you want when it comes to wine. Chances are, you aren't afraid to ask them to "hold the onions" or "put the dressing on the side." Wine requests might be asked a little less frequently, but good servers and good restaurants will want to accommodate you if you're gracious and polite.

Ordering by the Glass

If a restaurant tends to go through a high volume of wine and has a good size by-the-glass menu, don't hesitate to order by the glass. Ordering by the glass makes it easier to mix and match wines with courses, and it's easier to try different pairings and see how things match up.

If you're ordering by the glass, first decide if you want to pair your whole menu—your appetizer, salad, and entrée—with individual wines, or if you want to just get one glass that best matches the one dish and doesn't clash with the rest of your courses. The nice thing about ordering by the glass is you're free to switch wines, course to course, and it's fun to come up with your own pairing menus.

Some restaurants offer *wine flights*, which you can have a lot of fun with. You get to taste two or three wines, in smaller portions, and you'll be able to better discern which matches your dish.

If you are torn between two wines by the glass, ask if you can have a half portion, or a taste, of each. If both wines cost the same or roughly the same (or you're willing to be charged the more expensive amount if they don't cost the same), sometimes a restaurant will be willing to serve you two half portions. This is fun to do if you want to order wines for two different courses or if you want to try both wines with the same course to see if one tastes better with the dish.

> **def•i•ni•tion**
>
> **Wine flights** are typically made up of three half glasses of three different wines that have something in common. They might all be from the same region or made from the same grape, for example. Flights are a great way to experiment and try several new wines without breaking the bank.

Another option that is sometimes available is the half carafe or half bottle, which holds enough wine for about two to three glasses. They're really nice to share between two people, and sometimes, it's easier to order two different half bottles to see which wine goes better with your meals or courses.

> **Wine Nerd**
>
> If your server is particularly helpful, or goes above and beyond what is normally asked—such as serving you two half glasses of wine—be sure to tip accordingly.

Ordering by the Bottle

Sometimes, you just want to order a bottle of wine. It's a special dinner, and you're out with friends, and you want to split a bottle. Or you're at a restaurant that specializes in beer so you figure you'll have a better chance of enjoying the wine if you order it by the bottle.

When you're ordering to pair wine with food, wait until everyone has more or less decided what they want to order, and then decide whether your group wants one bottle for appetizers and salads, and another one for entrées—or a single bottle for the entire meal. A single bottle contains four to six glasses, depending on how large your pours are. If you are really careful, you can split a bottle of wine between 8 to 10 people, but just expect enough to taste.

If you plan on ordering two bottles, your job has just gotten a lot easier, especially if the entrées range from pork tenderloin with apples to rare ahi tuna with soba noodles, with steak with potatoes in between. In the case of two bottles, you can order one that pairs with meat entrées and one that goes with seafood or chicken entrées.

But if you're just going to order one bottle, you've got a conundrum. If your table prefers red wines in general, but a couple people are ordering lighter dishes, go with a lighter Pinot Noir or Beaujolais. It might not pair up perfectly with that steak, but chances are, it's not going to completely crush that chicken kiev, either. Rosés can be a good compromise when people at your table are ordering a variety of entrées, too.

But even if everyone's ordering fish at a seafood restaurant or meat at a steakhouse, that Sauvignon Blanc or big Cabernet might not work perfectly with every dish. In the case of everyone ordering something of a similar weight, but with different sauces and seasonings, sometimes the way to go is a white or red *blend*. Restaurants often carry blended wines, and these tend to work for a variety of different entrées. That's because chances are that one of the grapes in the blend has characteristics that match the nuances of your dish.

def•i•ni•tion

A **blend** or a **blended wine** is simply a wine that is made from more than one type of grape.

If you're in the company of people who really don't care about pairings, pick the wine that goes with your entrée. At least you'll be happy!

The Wine Serving Ritual

When you order a bottle of wine at a restaurant, it always seems like a big production. Although the serving ritual might appear stilted and stuffy, its purpose is to prevent mistakes, so when the server arrives at your table with bottle of wine in hand, stop your conversation and pay attention. Let's go through the process.

When the server or sommelier brings the wine to your table, they will present you (or whoever ordered the wine) with the bottle. That's to make sure that he or she has the right bottle. When the bottle is presented to you, read the label and check the year. Sometimes, a restaurant serves the same wine from more than one vintage year, and if you ordered a 2005 and got a 2007, it's important to say something because the price and quality could be much different from the one you ordered.

Another common mistake is for a server to bring a different varietal by the same winemaker—for instance you ordered the JJ Cellars Syrah but the server brought JJ Cellars Pinot Noir to the table. No matter what the mistake, it's a lot easier to fix the problem before the bottle is opened. All the server has to do is return the incorrect bottle to the cellar and bring back the right one.

> **Corked**
>
> Pay attention when the bottle is presented to your table and take the time to read the label. This will help you to correct a mistake before the bottle is opened.

Once you confirm that it is the correct bottle, the sommelier will open it and present you with the cork. Take a look at it. Is it stained all the way to the top, as though wine has seeped out of the bottle? Is it crumbly and falling apart? Is it completely dried out and shriveled? These all can be signs that the bottle wasn't stored properly, so you'll need to pay closer attention when smelling the wine.

As for smelling the cork, it is up to you, but we don't recommend it. Cork aromas can often be misleading.

Next, the sommelier will pour you a small sample: swirl it, look at it, sniff it. In short, go through the eight S's of wine tasting (see Chapter 2).

If it smells bad or tastes "off," it's a lot easier to voice your concern and have the bottle replaced at this point than it would be after everyone at the table already has a full glass.

Restaurants are typically a lot more willing to replace the bottle when only one small amount has been poured from it, than after everyone has had a glass. They can recork the bad bottle and return it to their distributor to receive credit for the bottle. If everyone's taken a drink, they can't send it back, and they're stuck paying for a bad bottle.

If the wine passes muster, give your server the nod. He or she will then proceed to pour everyone a glass of wine.

Wine Nerd

If the wine happens to be particularly stellar, a really nice thing to do is to offer the server or the sommelier a taste. While a sommelier has, most likely, tried all the wines by the glass, he or she probably has not tasted many of the more expensive bottles on the menu.

The proper way to do this is to offer a taste, and then to pour him or her an ounce or half-ounce portion. This is not only a real treat for the sommelier, but it also helps him or her do his or her job better. After having tasted it, he or she will better be able to pair that wine in the future. Think of it as a way of paying, or rather pouring, it forward.

If you've ordered wine by the glass, sometimes an inexperienced server or bartender will fill your glass too full, probably because the restaurant's glasses are too small. That means either you'll have to gulp down half your wine in order to swirl it in the glass or risk spilling some wine when you do swirl it. Don't hesitate to ask for an empty glass. You might get a weird look, but go ahead and ask anyway. You'll enjoy your wine experience much more if you can actually smell the wine before you sip it.

Enjoying a Chef's Menu

One of the best ways to learn more about wine and food pairings is to order the chef's menu—sometimes called the tasting menu, seasonal menu, or degustation menu—along with preselected wines paired with each course. Though chef's menus started out in only the finest of restaurants, today many good bistros and cafés offer them.

If you have the appetite for it and can afford it, likely the chef's menu is the best thing on the menu. It usually includes the chef's top dishes or seasonal favorites. The chef and the sommelier have put a lot of care and thought into the menu, and it is especially designed to have a progression of flavors and tastes.

> **Corked** _____
>
> Although restaurants will probably be willing to substitute items on the chef's menu if you suffer from a food allergy or a dietary restriction, they may not be as willing to make substitutions if you simply don't like a certain ingredient. If certain courses or sauces are partially prepared in advance, substitutions may be especially difficult.

Even if there is a course on the tasting menu that sounds too extreme for your tastes, we encourage you to be adventurous and order it anyway. You might be pleasantly surprised, and the only way for you to expand your palate is to try new things.

The nice thing about ordering a chef's menu is that you leave all the decisions to someone else. You put yourself in the chef and the sommelier's able hands, and enjoy your meal. If there's a stellar pairing that really sings to you, have the sommelier write it down. When you have returned from your food and wine–induced nirvana, put the notes in your wine journal so you can replicate the experience at home.

When Bad Wine Happens

Sometimes, no matter the caliber of the restaurant, no matter the overall quality of the service, bad wine just happens. You're poured a glass, and it smells off or tastes awful. You're awaiting a taste of that great bottle you ordered, and that great bottle turns out to be not so great.

Bad wine happens—even to the best of people and even when a restaurant really cares for its wines. When you encounter bad wine, you need to address the problem immediately.

If you're served a glass, signal (politely, of course!) the server, and tell him or her that the wine doesn't seem right. Sometimes, it's obvious— it's a Riesling that smells like gym socks or a Cabernet Sauvignon that has fizzy bubbles. When you say something, if the server gets surly and says "That's the way it is supposed to taste," be firm, but polite, and ask him or her to taste it to be sure.

When ordering by the glass, sometimes the bottles have been open too long and get oxidized. Sometimes, they're corked. If it tastes like vinegar, no matter what kind of wine, it's not good.

Corked

Wines that have Grenache grapes in them tend to oxidize more quickly than other wines. If the wine you want has Grenache in it—be it a Côte du Rhône or a Spanish blend—it's better to order it by the bottle rather than the glass. If you order it by the bottle, you'll know just how long the cork has been out and just how much air has gotten to the wine.

Keep in mind that big, heavy reds naturally smell oxidized or earthy. Old-World reds sometimes just have a bit of funk to them, in smell or taste, and that's usually terroir-based. Rhone reds can smell like a wet, mushroomy, forest floor, for instance, and Burgundian Pinot Noirs can smell like a barnyard. Sauvignon Blancs from the Loire Valley and New Zealand also sometimes have notes of "cat urine," and that really is how they're supposed to smell. But if it is a New-World red wine, it is very unlikely that it should intentionally smell or taste funky.

If you are served a bad wine, tell the server or sommelier, "I believe this wine is flawed." Then, offer the server, sommelier, or manager a taste to verify it.

It's always awkward when this happens, but it is best to address it immediately. If the wine is flawed—and not because it's a Bordeaux that happens to smell a bit like stinky beef jerky—they should try to remedy the situation.

It's right to expect that if you order a wine-by-the-glass that tastes bad, they will substitute it with a new glass. Similarly, if a bottle is obviously corked, it needs to be replaced. But don't expect them to buy your meal or dessert, and if they go out of their way to correct the situation, tip them accordingly.

Corked

If bad wine happens, address the situation immediately. Don't suffer through the glass or the bottle, then stew about it for a week, and then call or write a letter of complaint. Unless you asked for the situation to be corrected at the time, and everyone was downright rude to you, such complaints are unnecessary. It's best to address things right away when there's a better chance for them to be corrected.

The Least You Need to Know

- If the restaurant goes through a high volume of wines, ordering by the glass might be your best bet. If the restaurant doesn't specialize in wines, order a bottle.

- Ordering by the glass gives you more freedom to mix and match wines with courses.

- When the server presents the bottle to you, confirm that it is what you ordered.

- When ordering by the bottle for everyone, seek a middle ground when trying to match all the dishes at the table with that one bottle.

- Ordering from the chef's tasting menu is a great way to try the best items on the menu and have them paired perfectly with wines.

- Bad wine sometimes happens. Address the problem immediately and politely.

Chapter 16

Shopping for Wine and Planning a Pairing Party

In This Chapter

- Shopping for wine
- Grocery stores vs. wine shops
- The pros and cons of wine clubs
- Organizing a pairing party

Get out your credit card! This chapter covers all the wine shopping basics. You'll learn about the best—and not so ideal—places to get wine as well as how to get the most out of the staff.

And once you've bought all that wine, it's party time. You'll find tips for planning and pulling off a wine-pairing party, so you can apply all the pairing principles you've learned so far in this book.

In short, this chapter covers all of the fun stuff you will need to know to go forth and pair wine with food, and share it with others.

Where to Buy Your Wine

Just because a store sells wine, it doesn't mean they've cared for it properly or that it's going to be good wine.

Grocery Stores

Most run-of-the-mill grocery stores sell wine, and it may be convenient to grab a bottle while you are doing your grocery shopping. But if you're really looking to get that perfect wine to pair with your food, and if you like to get recommendations from a knowledgeable employee, then your standard grocery store likely won't be the place to shop for wine. The same is true of pharmacies with liquor departments. They may sell wine, but it's not necessarily going to be the kind of wine that you want.

If you need to pick up a quick bottle of red to go with the burgers your spouse is grilling, or if you're in a bind and need a bottle, then the grocery or pharmacy will probably do the trick. But know that you might be paying more for a lower-quality wine than you would at a specialty wine or liquor store, and know that you're not likely getting a great bottle.

You're not really going to find many highly rated bottles in a grocery store or pharmacy. You'll find some big bottles and boxes of wine, and the cheap imports that are advertised on billboards. But it's a grab n' go kind of place—not a place with a stellar selection. As a general rule, specialty stores offer better wine selections and service.

Some grocery stores do have good wine or liquor departments. Such stores are usually smaller and more gourmet-oriented, and the owner or wine buyer on staff—and often on the premises while you shop—has a say in what is purchased and put out on the shelves. Some specialty chain grocers like Whole Foods do a good job, and they have an educated staff. And some large wholesale stores like Costco and Sam's Club also do a more than adequate job at selling wine. In fact, Costco can be a pretty good place to find a good bargain. Trader Joe's does an all-right job for bulk, no-frills wines.

Wine Nerd

Trader Joe's is famous for its "2 Buck Chuck" or Charles Shaw labeled wines (which sell for around $2.99 a bottle). What's interesting to note is that if you liked the Charles Shaw Chardonnay last time you bought it, the next time you buy it, it might not be the same wine at all. Charles Shaw, owned by Bronco Wine Co., purchases surplus wine from a wide variety of other wineries, so it's never the same wine twice.

Wine Shops

Our hands-down favorite place to purchase wine is from the "little guys." We recommend going to a good wine shop or a liquor store that has a good selection of wines. In addition to having a good selection of quality wines, these stores will almost always have a knowledgeable staff.

How can you tell if a wine shop or a liquor store is good? First, how do they treat you as a customer? At a good store, if you're wandering around the aisles, it won't take long before someone asks if they can help you. Second, if you approach them for assistance, they're happy to help you—they won't look at you with disdain when you ask for help choosing a decent bottle of wine for under $10, for instance. Third, you'll probably learn something when you shop there.

Good wine and liquor stores often do not shelve all of their wines or spirits. Like a fine art museum, they've got a deep inventory, some of which is in back. That's why, if you're looking for a specific wine, ask. If it's not on the shelf, that doesn't mean it's not in the store. Chances are they will either have it, be able to special order it, or steer you toward another, equally fine choice.

Becoming a regular at a wine shop is not a bad thing. In fact, if you get to know the staff, and they get to know you, they'll be able to tell you when something new comes in that they think you may be interested in. It

Wine Nerd

We've actually been in stores that have secret rooms and special conveyor belts and contraptions in which they bring up the special wine you've requested or ordered. It's fun to watch and makes getting that special bottle even more exciting.

also never hurts to sign up for their newsletters or e-mail alerts—these typically inform customers of special deals, new arrivals, bulk purchases, wines of the week, and so on.

Many wine shops offer special tastings, and these are definitely worth attending. For little or no charge you'll get to taste a variety of wines, including some expensive ones you wouldn't want to purchase without trying first. It's a good way to educate yourself further about wine. Some shops even offer classes and clubs, and those can be good educational opportunities, too.

Getting Your Wine through Wine Clubs and Other Venues

Wineries, private groups, and even newspapers like *The Wall Street Journal*, offer wine clubs these days. Clubs can be good places to get wine, but you have to understand how they work.

Wine clubs typically fall into one of two categories—those that send you wines as they are released and charge only for the wines that ship, or those that charge a flat rate and send you a bottle or two every month or so. In both cases, you're going to get good wine at a reduced rate. In the case of a winery-run wine club, very often you get extra perks such as being invited to special open houses and having the tasting fee waived in the tasting room. The costs, number of bottles received, and frequency of shipping depends on each wine club. They usually cost $30 and up per month. If you are adventurous, this is a great way to try new things, but if you like to have more control or think you'll send a lot of bottles back (and return policies vary from club to club), then this is not for you.

Whether you go with a club through a winery or through a specialty wine shop or group, a wine club offers you a way to let others do the work for you. Good clubs may even send recipes and pairing suggestions with each wine.

Some companies and wine stores offer in-home tastings for a fee, or even free, if you order a certain amount of wine. This can be fun and you can even use this service as a chance to throw a wine party for friends and relatives.

These companies usually ask you about your wine preferences ahead of time and offer wines that you might not find in a store because they often purchase from smaller, boutique wineries. These are sort of like Tupperware parties for wine and offer you a chance to try new wines before you buy.

Corked

Whether in-home parties and wine clubs are an option for you depends on your state's laws regarding alcohol distribution.

Perfect Pairings

Another way to purchase wine is through wine dinners. You can often purchase wine at special wine dinners held at a restaurant. This is usually the best place to get the best price for a special bottle or two. Keep in mind that the wineries that participate in such dinners usually donate the wines to the dinner, and they only make money on the bottles sold at the meal. So if you like the wine and plan to buy it, help out the winery by purchasing the wine at the dinner.

How to Shop for Wine

No matter where you shop, you're still going to need to go into the store with a game plan. The first thing you need to know is who or what you are buying the wine for.

If you're buying it for an in-law who is just as happy sipping wine coolers, then maybe you don't want to get a $20 bottle for dinner. If you're purchasing it for your friends who tend to overindulge, ditto. But if you're planning a dinner party for friends or relatives who care about what they drink, then you'll probably want to splurge a little bit more.

If you are planning to pair your wine with a meal, then bring along a list of the courses as well as their ingredients. This will help the clerk at the store steer you toward the right wines.

Be sure to set a budget before you set foot into the store so you don't end up spending more than you wanted. While you can occasionally find some steals at $10 or less per bottle, in general, plan on spending $15 for a good bottle of wine. You should be able to purchase a very good bottle of wine for anywhere from $15 to $40. Any time you spend more than $40, the wine had better be stellar. If you pay $50 or more, it better knock your socks off.

Just because a bottle is more expensive doesn't mean that it's going to actually be a better wine. That's why, if you're planning on spending more on a bottle, it's best if you taste it first, either at a restaurant or at a tasting event. You will want to know for sure if the bottle is what you want.

Corked

Anytime that you're going to shell out $50 or more for a wine, make sure it is a good bottle. Check the bottle for any signs of poor storage, like wine stains on the label or an unusually low amount of wine in the bottle. Also, make sure it is a wine you will enjoy. There are perfectly good bottles of expensive wine that might not suit your palate.

If you're doing a more experimental pairing, it's a good idea to have a backup wine. Buy that crazy wine, but get a more traditional bottle to have in reserve, just in case the pairing doesn't work. Like the Boy Scouts, wine lovers should always be prepared.

Wine Nerd

Because both of us believe in being prepared for all occasions, we both keep bottles of our "house red" and "house white" in our cellar. These house wines should cost no more than $15. Jaclyn always has six bottles of Chardonnay and six bottles of Pinot Noir on hand. Jeanette keeps a stash of four varied whites and four varied reds. Not only for pairings that don't work, but also for that last minute hostess gift or unexpected house guest. Having these fail-safe wines on hand keeps us from parting with the wines that we truly adore in our cellars. When your stash gets low, replenish it.

Pairing Party Planning 101

Wine parties are a lot of fun, and wine and food pairing parties are even more enjoyable. If you're planning on hosting a wine and food tasting party with the goal of coming up with some great pairs, there are a couple of ways to approach your party.

Who Supplies the Wine and Food?

You can pick out all the wines yourself and supply all of the food, or you can invite your guests to contribute a bottle of wine, a dish to share, or both. You might consider inviting your guests to bring a bottle and a dish they think pairs well with it. Then, you can mix and match dishes and wines.

It might be fun to pick a theme, such as Italian reds or Sauvignon Blancs from around the globe. Themes also make it easier to plan the food, especially if you're providing all of the eats. They are also more educational for both you and your guests. If you are tasting different winemakers' versions of one varietal or a number of wines from one wine region, rather than a wide variety of wines from a number of different regions, you'll be better able to discern small differences, thus educating your palate.

Whether you provide all the wine or your guests bring bottles, you'll have to decide whether to serve it straight out of the bottles or do blind tastings. If you opt for blind tastings, you'll need to hide the labels. You can do this by putting the bottles in brown lunch bags or wrapping the bottles in aluminum foil. Aluminum foil is a lot less messy and makes for easier pouring, but it does show off the shape of the bottle, which can, oddly enough, affect people's opinions.

Corked

If you are asking guests to bring wine and you do not have a theme, assign whites to one group of guests and reds to another; otherwise, you might end up with five bottles of Riesling and not much else. This is exactly what happened to Jeanette when she threw a surprise wine-tasting birthday party for her husband.

Perfect Pairings

To further educate your palate and those of your guests, set up an aromatics tasting to better learn about the aromas of wines.

When deciding how much wine you need, plan on 2 ounces per wine per person, if you're tasting a variety of wines. If you're doing a sit-down meal, plan for about 5 ounces of wine per person.

With any wine party, you usually have two goals—to educate yourselves and to socialize. It's up to you which of the goals is more important.

If education is a priority, you might consider hiring a sommelier or a staff person from your favorite wine shop, especially if you are picking out all the wines yourself. Such a professional will charge anywhere from $50 to $300, depending on how much time is involved, in addition to the cost of the wines.

While it may cost you more in one sense, it saves you money and time. Very often, these professionals will come with printed materials, and even bring in their own wine glasses for the tasting, so you don't have to purchase supplies or extra crystal for the event. And you won't have any glasses to wash afterward.

That brings us to the next part of party planning: equipment.

The Right Tools for a Righteous Party

Though you can buy plastic wine glasses—the ones that are popular just before New Year's Eve—for a wine party, we don't recommend doing so. A big part of enjoying wine is enjoying its aromas, and you're never going to get the most out of a wine's aromas if you're drinking it from a plastic cup.

You definitely want to go with glass wine glasses, but you don't have to pull out your precious crystal stemware for a large group, and you don't necessarily have to serve everyone in the same glasses. Estate sales, garage sales, and thrift stores all sell nice wine glasses at reasonable prices. If you're serving red wines, try to have red wine glasses that are similar so that everyone has a comparable tasting experience. But they don't have to be exactly alike.

You can also host a BYOG—or Bring Your Own Glass—party. That way everyone has their own glass that, presumably, they will be happy with. If you really want to provide all the glassware and have it all match, you can rent glasses from a local party supply shop or caterer.

It's hard to sip and eat if you don't have at least one hand free, so you might want to consider buying plates that snap onto the stem of a wine glass or plate clips, which attach the plates to the glasses. This frees up a hand so you can jot down notes about all those great, and not-so-great, pairings. Plus, they make it easier to mingle, and they're especially handy if you're serving small hors d'oeuvres or tapas. In addition, you'll need napkins and the proper silverware for the food you're serving.

Unless you expect your guests to like every wine and drink every last drop poured in their glasses, you'll need spit buckets. But instead of buying actual spit buckets, you can get away with using a variety of vases—again, something you can pick up at the thrift store—or try children's sand pails. Just make sure the buckets or vases aren't clear or see-through: no one wants to see wine and spit.

 Corked

If you use children's pails as spit buckets, don't carry them by the handle to empty them. Doing so causes the contents to slosh around, and you might end up with a spill.

Since the goal of a tasting party is to learn more about wines give copies of tasting sheets to your guests, or distribute index cards for the same purpose. If you want to make it even more memorable, pick up some cheap photo albums from the dollar store to give to people to store their index cards in as a keepsake.

Be sure to serve plenty of water. It's good for cleansing the palate, rinsing your glass, and maintaining sobriety. Bottled water or filtered water is best—the minerals in tap water can adversely affect the taste of wine.

Finally, whip up some wine cleaner, and have it on hand to clean up any spills on your carpet or furniture.

Corked

Don't wear white or light clothes to wine tastings. The Murphy's Law of wine tasting is if you wear a white shirt, you will spill red wine on it.

If you're concerned about spills and such, consider renting out a community center or a wine store for your event. Many stores host such events after hours, and it makes the cleanup a lot easier on your part.

The Least You Need to Know

◆ Wine shops and liquor stores that specialize in wine offer better service and selections than most grocery stores.

◆ Wine clubs can be a good deal for wine purchases.

◆ Keep in mind who or what you're buying the wine for when shopping, and set a budget before you go.

◆ Bring a detailed list of courses and ingredients when trying to pair them up with wine.

◆ Parties often are both social and educational. If the purpose is mostly educational, consider hiring a sommelier to "up the educational ante" at the party.

◆ Make sure you have real glasses, spit buckets, and plates that can be attached to glasses for a party.

Chapter

17

Pairing Beer, Spirits, Coffee, and Tea

In This Chapter

◆ Pairing beer

◆ Pairing spirits

◆ Pairing tea and coffee

Now that you understand the basics of pairing wine with food, you can take that knowledge and apply it to other beverages, including beer, spirits, tea, and coffee. Basic wine-pairing principles such as "goes with where it grows," and "red goes with red, white goes with white" can also be applied to these other beverages.

You can apply what you know about wine to other beverages, drawing on the same tools you use to taste and pair wine.

Pairing Beer with Food

People have been consuming beer alongside food for ages. In fact, many think the first beverage—after water, of course—was likely some form of beer. But even though we've been drinking beer and eating food together for a millennia, chefs have only recently discovered the art of the beer dinner.

Beer dinners are becoming quite haute and humble ales are being served alongside extravagant dishes; this is an exciting thing for beer lovers. Restaurants have even started featuring "beer dinners," just like their wine dinner counterpart.

Beer has many parallels to wine, and the process of pairing beer with food is similar to wine and food pairing. As a matter of fact, one of the most basic wine-pairing rules—"goes with where it grows"—works just as well with beers. Countries that make a lot of beer serve cuisine that pairs up nicely with the local beers.

German, English, and Japanese cuisines all pair up quite nicely with beer, so do Irish, Belgian, and Mexican cuisines. But just as there are many different types of grape varietals, there are a lot of different types of beer.

Wine Nerd

Beer is made from four basic ingredients: yeast, hops, malted barley, and water. Most beer can be divided into one of three types: ales, lagers, and specialty beers, and within specialty beers, you'll find beers made with extra ingredients. The difference between the ales and lagers is the type of yeast used.

Within each category, the beer types are further divided. Ales include: barley wine, English bitter, pale ales, Scottish ales, Belgian ales, porters, and stouts. Within lagers, you'll find: pilsners, bocks, American lagers (including light beers), Oktoberfest brews, helles, and dunkels. Specialty beers include: weizenbier (wheat beers), smoked beers, fruit beers, and spice beers.

Another wine-pairing rule you can borrow when pairing beers is "red goes with red, white goes with white." Lighter beers pair up better with lighter meats and seafood; darker or heavier beers pair better with heavier meats.

And if you're planning to drink beer with a dish that has a sauce or gravy, add beer to the sauce to improve the pairing. Cooking with beer is a wonderful thing, and you can even add beer to your desserts.

> ### Wine Nerd
>
> A good website to check out if you want to cook with beer is www.beercook.com. Lucy Saunders, the author of the site, is quite knowledgeable.

Beer also has aromas, and you can read the label to figure out pairings. For example, Oberon by Bell's Brewery is often served with a wedge of orange so if you're serving duck à l'orange, it would make a good pair. If you're pouring a seasonal pumpkin brew, enjoy it with another autumnal dish such as wild rice stuffed squash.

Another thing to keep in mind is that the hoppier the beer is, the more bitter it will be. Hops are beer's equivalent of tannins, so when you pair a hoppy ale, you want to pair it with something that can stand up to the hops, such as a steak or other meaty dish.

Beer, in general, also likes salt and fat. It's quite similar to sparkling wines that way. That's why bar food often contains copious amounts of both, and that's why mozzarella sticks and wings taste so good with beer!

Pairing Spirits with Food

Pairing spirits with food can be tricky. Unlike wine and beer, spirits were not designed to be consumed with food at the same time. They were, instead, designed to be savored before or after a meal. Their high alcohol content makes it far easier to become inebriated quickly.

Sobriety aside, this higher alcohol content needs to be considered when pairing spirits with food. Because of their heat, spirits, liquors, and cordials really shouldn't be paired with spicy foods. It's like adding fuel to the fire: it will put a spicy, Mexican salsa into overdrive, turn a Thai curry into a raging fire, and make your hot wings inferno-hot.

Perfect Pairings

You can tone down the heat of the spirit with the addition of some juice or cream, but then you have created a cocktail. When pairing cocktails, you need to consider the main flavors and aromas, not just the spirit itself, and pair them with complimentary or similar foods.

Spirits were developed with the intent to be sipped and savored slowly and were not made to be paired with food. But they do make marvelous additions to recipes.

Bourbon goes really well in barbecue sauces, whiskey can deglaze a pan, and brandies add a hint of sweetness to cream sauces. As with cooking with wine or beer, the alcohol will cook off, unless it is added after the cooking process (which is often the case with desserts such as rum cakes). Any recipe that contains a spirit as an ingredient can be paired with such spirits or cocktails that contain them. Another thing to keep in mind is that spirits that have been barrel-aged often have a hint of smoke on the nose, so they pair well with equally smoky barbecued or smoked foods. Individual spirits have different flavor profiles, which must be considered when pairing.

Gin

Gin is a particularly herbaceous spirit. In fact, some gins have a very distinct flavor. Hendricks has cucumber notes, while Rehorst, made by a Milwaukee *craft distiller*, tastes of basil. Served straight or in a cocktail, they can pair up well with dishes that feature these herbs and notes.

def•i•ni•tion

A **craft distiller** makes spirits in small batches by hand. Craft distilleries are popping up across the country, and they make some really inventive and delicious spirits.

A cucumber salad goes great with a Hendricks martini; a basil and tomato salad goes great with a Rehorst cocktail. If you infuse the cocktail further with actual cucumbers or basil, the herbal notes become even more pronounced.

Vodka

Vodka, unlike gin, tends to be a more neutral spirit. If it is made with potatoes, however, it will pair up nicely with potato dishes. It also goes great with blue or fresh chèvre cheeses (cheese-stuffed olives in martinis, anyone?), and it is amazing with delicate dishes like caviar.

Rum

Rum is traditionally served in tropical drinks, and it goes with tropical, sweet and sour dishes. Dark rums, which have notes of caramel, also pair up wonderfully with caramel-laced desserts.

Cordials

Cordials often have notes of fruit, nuts, or herbs. They're typically served as a digestif or an after dinner drink. As such, if you're drinking peach liquor, pair it with a peach cobbler. Frangelico tastes amazing when paired with a hazelnut torte, and Chambord goes great with a raspberry sorbet.

Since cordials are sweet, you can go one-step further and drizzle them right on the desserts themselves. A little goes a long way, but they really do enhance a dessert.

Cordial cocktails also pair well with desserts. Kahlua-based drinks such as white Russians taste oh-so-good with chocolate brownies. Grand Marnier cocktails go great with citrus desserts, including dark chocolate flourless cake topped with orange wedges.

Perfect Pairings

A very simple way to enhance a plain dessert is to add a bit of cordial to it. Vanilla ice cream, pound cake, and plain cheesecake can all be enhanced with a drizzle of Chambord, schnapps, or Kahlua. And, it will be a perfect pair with your cordial.

Sake

Though not exactly a spirit, sakes are a wonderful, and often over-looked, beverage to pair with food. Considered "rice wine," sake is tra-ditionally served with Japanese cuisine. Its starchy quality lends itself to pairing with all sorts of rice dishes.

Although there are at least 70 different kinds of sake, here are the main types: Honjõzõ, Junmai, Ginjõ, and Daiginjõ. These main styles are defined by the amount that the rice grains have been polished prior to fermentation. This polishing removes proteins and oils, leaving only the fermentable starch behind.

Honjõzõ is the term for bulk sakes and aren't recommended for pairing. Junmai, Ginjõ, and Daiginjõ are in order of increased polishing, and thus boast an increasing quality and complexity. Junmai is typically sweetest, and is best with spicy and sweet foods like bean paste dump-lings. Ginjõ and Daiginjõ are much dryer and more subtle, and are better paired with savory, yet delicate dishes like sushi and sashimi. In general, sake pairs better with more delicate dishes because the bever-age's subtle qualities will get lost when paired with heavier foods.

Sake is best enjoyed cold, and it is best served within six months of bot-tling. Because it turns so quickly, it's best to purchase your sake from a place that goes through a higher volume than your typical liquor store. Some Asian, and in particu-lar Japanese, grocery stores stock fresher, quality sakes, so you're less likely to get stuck with a bottle that has been sitting on the shelves for years. Most quality sakes have a bot-tling date stamp or label, so be sure to check the bottle before you buy.

> **Wine Nerd**
>
> Mitsuwa Marketplace is a great Japanese grocery store, and it has five locations in the United States. Visit www.mitsuwa.com.

Pairing Tea and Coffee with Food

Foodies have become increasingly interested in pairing teas and cof-fees with foods. In fact, a recent American Cheese Society conference offered a seminar on pairing coffee and cheese! While it might seem a bit odd to pair tea and coffee with foods other than brunch or dessert, you might be surprised by—and delighted with—some of the interesting combinations you can come up with.

Tea

Tea has many similarities to wine. Like wine, it contains tannins and is a complex beverage. Tea generally falls into one of four categories: white, green, black, or oolong. There's also pu-erh, rooibos, and herbal teas, which are also known as botanical blends.

On the intensity scale, white is the least intense, followed in order by green, black, and oolong. They are each processed differently, and the tea leaves are oxidized in a different manner. Pu-erh is a special type of tea that is often fermented (and is thus, often quite strong). Rooibos or red tea is a caffeine-free herb from Africa that is light and sweet. Herbal teas or botanical blends are caffeine-free blends of herbs, spices, and fruits and aren't really teas at all, since they do not contain any tea leaves.

In general, think of white and lighter green teas as white wines, and think of black and oolong teas as red wines. Aged or fermented pu-erh teas can also be considered as red wines because of their complexity. Rooibos teas can be considered light rosés, not only because of their color, but also because of their intensity. Herbal teas and botanical blends must be considered on an individual basis; they are too varied in intensity to classify into any one group.

All types of tea can be blended with spices, fruits, and herbs. For pairing purposes you can sometimes match the spice with the food. A strawberry-laced, white tea goes quite well with a strawberry shortcake, for example. A lemon meringue pie goes great with a lemon-laced tea.

In tastings, one tea Jeanette discovered to be quite versatile in pairing with food is jasmine green tea. Light and floral, it is reminiscent of a food-friendly Riesling. Jasmine green tea pairs well with chèvre, rice dishes, and seafoods.

In any tea pairing or tea service in general, it is important to brew the tea with filtered water at the proper time and temperature. Minerals in tap water can adversely affect the tea.

Teas can also be added to sauces and gravies, and they can deglaze pans, too. The thing to keep in mind when cooking with tea is that you have to brew it at the right temperature and then blend it with your food. Tea-scented desserts and pastries—especially scones—are downright heavenly.

Coffee

Like tea, coffee has numerous types of roasts and blends. But even the lightest of coffee roasts tend to have a higher amount of tannin and bitterness than tea.

Bitterness in coffee is something that you will want to keep in mind while pairing. Because of its bitterness, it is traditionally served at the end of the meal (which typically progresses from light to heavy foods), and it is most often served with something sweet.

The sweetness in desserts and baked goods pair up smashingly with coffee's bitterness. Creamy desserts—panna cotta, cheesecake, crème brûlée, and ice cream—all work very, very well with coffee.

Coffee purists take it black and straight up, but the rest of us sometimes want a little cream or sugar in it, and we also love espresso-based drinks. Espresso-based drinks often have flavorings in them, and for pairing purposes, pair with the flavor. A honey latte goes great with a honey dessert like baklava, for example.

You can also add coffee to sauces, gravies, and, of course, desserts like tiramisu. This is the easiest way to pair coffee—use the same coffee you cooked with.

Pairing with Other Beverages

Fruit juices, sodas, and even waters can be paired with foods. The general wine-pairing rules work with these beverages, too.

The main thing you will want to do when pairing other beverages is to think aromas and intensity. Match the aromas and the intensity of the beverages with the food, and chances are you'll have a good match. And as always, have fun with your pairing.

The Least You Need to Know

- ◆ Two wine-pairing rules that apply almost as well with beer are, "goes with where it grows," and "red goes with red, white goes with white."

- ◆ Never pair spirits with spicy foods, their high alcohol content will add flames to the fire.

- ◆ Try to match the different aromas or flavors of spirits and cordials with the dishes. A peach schnapps goes well with a peach cobbler.

- ◆ Sake can be paired with a variety of different foods, like wine. But, unlike wine, it is best paired with more delicate flavors so that its own subtleties will shine through.

- ◆ Treat white and light green teas as you would white wines; treat black, oolong, and pu-erh teas as you would red wines.

- ◆ Coffee pairs particularly well with sweet desserts and baked goods because of its bitterness.

Glossary

appellation   A designated vineyard growing area specified by a local or national government.

aromatics   The fragrances in wine that are derived from a grape's varietal character.

austere   Used to describe a wine that is young and tannic.

biodynamic   A type of organic farming that takes into account the lunar cycles and works in harmony with the land.

blend   A wine that is made from more than one grape varietal.

blind tasting   An unbiased form of tasting; tasting wine without knowing anything about it, such as the winery, grape, or vintage.

body   The weight and mouthfeel of a wine.

Bordeaux   A region in France known for producing wines from primarily Cabernet Sauvignon and Merlot.

botrytized   Refers to the process of cultivating grapes so that a special mold called *botrytis cinera* grows on the grapes.

bouquet   The complex fragrances that develop in wine as a result of barrel or bottle aging.

Burgundy   A region in France known for producing wines from Pinot Noir and Chardonnay grapes.

Champagne   A region in France known for producing sparkling wines.

Chianti   A region in Tuscany, Italy, known for producing red wine made from predominantly Sangiovese grapes.

corked   Wine that has been exposed to bad bacteria that has spoiled its inherent goodness, making it smell like wet cardboard.

cuvée   Means "blend" in French and refers to the specific blend of varietals used to create a specific sparkling wine.

decanting   The practice of pouring wine from the bottle into a secondary serving bottle in order to remove sediment or aerate it.

fining   A wine-making process in which a coagulant is added to the wine to collect any undesirable particles. Wines that are not "vegan" utilize egg whites or gelatin for this process.

finish   A wine's aftertaste. Often a wine's quality is measured by the length of its finish.

ice wines   Wines in which the grapes are left on the vine so long that they freeze, causing the grape to lose moisture and intensify the remaining sugar and flavor. They are known as *Eisweins* in Germany and Austria.

intensity   Description of a wine's sweetness, acid, and alcohol content.

lees   Yeast cells that have died after fermentation. Wines aged on the lees have extra flavor and body.

locavore   Someone who tries to eat mostly local foods, often grown within a 100-mile radius of his or her home.

New World   The part of the world that is "newer" to making wine; comprised of North and South America, Australia, and New Zealand.

oak   Type of wood used in wine barrels; it imparts more flavor, body, and tannin to wine.

oenology   The study of wine.

oenophiles   Fancy way to say "wine lovers."

Old World   The part of the world that has a long history of wine-making; comprised of European nations like France, Italy, Germany, Spain, Portugal, and Austria.

organic   A practice of farming that uses no chemical pesticides, herbicides, or fertilizers.

oxidized wine   Wine that has been exposed to air for too long, making it go stale.

raisinate   The process of leaving grapes on the vine after they are ripe, to dry in the sun like raisins.

residual sugar   The amount of sugar left in wine after fermentation.

Scoville scale   The scale used to measure the amount of heat in a hot pepper.

sediment   A naturally occurring deposit found in wines that are either unfiltered or aged.

sommelier   A certified restaurant employee or wine professional who is in charge of all things wine, especially creating wine and food pairings.

sparkling wine   Any wine with bubbles.

Stelvin closure   A "screw cap" on a bottle of wine.

structure   A term used to describe the overall tannin and acidity of a wine.

sugar   The compound utilized by yeast during fermentation to create alcohol.

tannin   Bitter compounds found in grape skins, seeds, and stalks that can create a dry, chalky, or puckered feeling in your mouth.

terroir   French term that denotes the effects that geography and distinct environments have on food products, particularly wine and cheese.

texture   The mouthfeel of a wine.

umami   Often called the "fifth taste"; a flavor that doesn't neatly fall into the categories of sweet, salty, sour, and bitter.

varietal   A specific grape type, like Cabernet Sauvignon or Pinot Gris.

vintage   The year the grapes were grown for a specific bottling.

volatile acidity or **VA**   When the acidity of a wine is so out of balance that it ruins the overall taste of the wine.

wine   Alcoholic beverage made from the fermented juice of grapes.

wine flights   Samples of wine sharing some common bond and typically served by restaurants in three half glasses.

yeast   The living microorganism that is necessary for making wine. Yeasts consume sugar to create alcohol, heat, and carbon dioxide.

Appendix 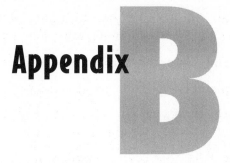 B

Tasting Journal

Copy this template to make your own wine and food pairing journal, or use it as a model to create your own notes.

Date: _____

Wine

Winery Name: _____

Name of Wine: _____ Price: $_____

Grape(s): _____

Region: _____ Vintage: _____

Alcohol: ___Low (<10%) ___Medium (10-13.5%) ___High (>14%)

Acidity: ____Low   ____Medium   ____High

Tannin: ____Low   ____Medium   ____High

Body: ____Light   ____Medium   ____Full

Bubbles: ____None   ____Frizzante   ____Fine   ____Large

Aromas/Bouquet: _____ _____ _____

_____ _____ _____ _____

Food

Name of Dish: _____

Cooking Method: _____ Intensity: _____Light _____Heavy

Primary Flavors: _____ _____ _____

Pairing

How did the food and wine interact? _____

_____

_____

Was this pairing successful? Why/Why not? _____Yes   _____No

_____

Master Pairings List

Antipasto plate (assorted salami, cheese, and olives)   Dry rosé, Pinot Grigio

Apple pie   Late harvest white wine, Madeira, Moscato d'Asti

Babyback ribs   Riesling, Shiraz, Zinfandel

Bagel with cream cheese and lox   Sparkling wine

Baked beans   Zinfandel, Cabernet Franc, Nebbiolo

Baked rigatoni with bolognese   Sangiovese, Cabernet Sauvignon, Zinfandel

Bean burrito/chimichanga   Red Rhone wines, Pinot Noir

Beef bourguignon   French Pinot Noir, Rhone reds

Beef carpaccio with garlic aioli   Dry rosés, Nebbiolo, rosé Champagne

Beef stir-fry   Zinfandel, Syrah/Shiraz

Beef stroganoff   Rhone Red, Nebbiolo, dry rosé

Beef tacos   South American Cabernet Sauvignon, Tempranillo, Verdejo

Beignets/donuts   Sparkling wine, Moscato d'Asti, Vin Santo

Blue cheese bacon burgers Zinfandel, Cabernet Sauvignon, Malbec

Bouillabaisse Dry rosé, Chardonnay

Bratwurst Off-dry Riesling, Zinfandel, Rhone reds

Brownies PX Sherry, Tawny Port (especially with nutty brownies)

Buffalo wings Sweet Riesling, Moscato d'Asti, Zinfandel

Caesar salad Pinot Grigio, sparkling wine, Sauvignon Blanc, Chardonnay

Cajun shrimp Off-dry Riesling or Gewürztraminer

Caprese salad Dry rosé, sparkling wine

Carrot cake Tokaji, sweet Gewürztraminer, Muscat

Cassoulet Rhone reds, dry rosés

Ceviche Albariño, Sauvignon Blanc, dry rosé, sparkling wine

Chicken Parmigiano Sangiovese, sparkling wine

Chicken potpie Sparkling wine, Chardonnay, Beaujolais

Chile relleno Off-dry Gewürztraminer or Riesling, Sauvignon Blanc, demi-sec or sweeter sparkling wine

Chili Zinfandel, Beaujolais

Chocolate mousse Tawny Port, Muscat, Vin Santo

Chorizo Off-dry Riesling, Tempranillo, Pinotage

Club sandwich Unoaked Chardonnay, Oregon Pinot Noir, sparkling wine

Cole slaw Unoaked Chardonnay, sparkling wine, Beaujolais

Corned beef and cabbage Pinot Blanc, Beaujolais, sparkling wine, green beer

Crab cakes Chardonnay, dry Riesling, Viognier, sparkling wine

Crawfish (boiled) Chardonnay, Chenin Blanc, sparkling wine

Crêpes (fruit) Sparkling wine, Moscato d'Asti

Crêpes (savory) Sparkling wine, Pinot Blanc, Chardonnay

Crème brûlée Sherry, late harvest white wines, demi-sec or sweeter Champagnes

Crudités Grüner Veltliner, Sauvignon Blanc, Pinot Blanc

Curried chicken Chardonnay, Gewürztraminer, sparkling wine

Duck confit French Malbec, Pinot Noir, Rhone reds, off-dry Riesling

Éclairs Sparkling Shiraz, sweet Sherry, Tawny Port

Egg rolls Sparkling wine, Pinot Blanc, Pinot Noir

Enchiladas Gewürztraminer, Verdejo, Petite Sirah

Fish and chips Sparkling wine, Pinot Gris/Grigio, dry rosé

Fried chicken Sparkling wine, unoaked Chardonnay, Sangiovese

French fries Sparkling wine, Chardonnay

Fruit salad Prosecco, Moscato d'Asti, off-dry Riesling or Gewürztraminer

Gazpacho French Sauvignon Blanc, dry Sherry

Greek salad Dry rosé, Sauvignon Blanc

Grilled cheese sandwich Chardonnay, Beaujolais

Gyros Dry rosés, Pinot Gris/Grigio, Gewürztraminer

Hot dog with sauerkraut Dry Riesling or Gewürztraminer

Hummus Sauvignon Blanc, Pinot Gris/Grigio, dry rosé

Jamaican jerk chicken Off-dry Riesling, rosés, sparkling wine

Jambalaya Chenin Blanc, off-dry Gewürztraminer, Tempranillo, Syrah

Lasagna Sangiovese, Pinot Noir

Lobster bisque Dry or off-dry Sherry, Chardonnay

Macaroni and cheese Pinot Grigio, Chardonnay, sparkling wine, Pinot Noir (with addition of blue cheese to the dish)

Meat loaf Merlot, Cabernet Sauvignon, Sangiovese

Mushroom risotto   Pinot Noir, Barbera, Pinot Grigio

New England clam chowder   Chardonnay, sparkling wine, Sherry

Nicçoise salad   Dry rosé, Sauvignon Blanc

Omelets   Sparkling wine; aged white wine, especially Pinot Blanc, white Rhone, and Chardonnay

Osso Bucco   Nebbiolo, Dolcetto, Syrah, Cabernet Sauvignon

Pad Thai   Sweet Riesling or Gewürztraminer

Paella   Dry rosé, Viognier, Verdejo, Tempranillo, dry Sherry

Pancakes and waffles with maple syrup   Sparkling wines, especially sparkling Shiraz

Pâté   Beaujolais, late harvest white wines

Pepperoni pizza   Sangiovese, Malbec, Barbera, dry rosé

Pierogies   Dry Riesling, Chardonnay

Popcorn, buttered   Chardonnay, sparkling wine

Pork chops   Gewürztraminer, Pinot Noir

Pork tamales   Gewürztraminer, Riesling, Tempranillo

Potato salad   Dry rosé, Sauvignon Blanc, Pinot Gris

Pumpkin ravioli   French Sauvignon Blanc, Chardonnay, Viognier

Rack of lamb   Shiraz, Merlot, Cabernet Sauvignon, Zinfandel

Ratatouille   Dry rosé

Rotisserie chicken   Oaked Chardonnay, Pinot Noir, Sangiovese

Salmon, grilled   South American Chardonnay, dry rosé, Pinot Noir

Shrimp scampi   Unoaked Chardonnay, Pinot Gris/Grigio, Prosecco

Spaghetti alla carbonara   Pinot Blanc, Pinot Gris/Grigio, dry rosé

Spaghetti with meatballs   Sangiovese, Montepulciano, Merlot

Spinach salad with hot bacon dressing   Pinot Noir, French Chardonnay

Surf and turf   Pinot Noir, dry rosé

Sweet potato casserole   Sweet Sherry, off-dry Riesling, Gewürztraminer

Sweetbreads   Pinot Noir, Chardonnay, sparkling wine

Tandoori chicken   Gewürztraminer, Shiraz, Zinfandel

Teriyaki beef   Zinfandel

Truffle mashed potatoes   Chardonnay, Pinot Noir, Nebbiolo

Tuna tartare   Pinot Noir

Veggie burgers   Dry rosé, oaked Sauvignon Blanc, Merlot

Venison, grilled   Syrah/Shiraz, Zinfandel, Rhone reds

Vichyssoise   French Sauvignon Blanc, dry Sherry

Wiener schnitzel   Grüner Veltliner, sparkling wine, Beaujolais

D

A Sampling of Chefs' Wine Menus

This appendix is intended to give you ideas to use in your own food and wine pairing events and meals.

The Menus

The following menus run from casual and every day, to extravagant and once-in-a-lifetime. We encourage you to be creative and use our ideas to inspire you to create your own pairing masterpieces.

You may notice that some menus list the wine first and others list the food first. Some pair multiple wines with one course and others with no wine at all. These variations are simply due to a restaurant or chef's personal style or preference, and what they thought was best to showcase the wine.

We have added a brief "why it works" explanation for each menu to give you a sense of what the chefs and sommeliers may have been thinking as they designed the menu. This should help you adapt the pairings to create your own personal pairing experiences.

Informal Home Party Featuring One Wine

This is an example of how to pair one wine to an entire meal.

Wine:

- ◆ Chateau Lestrille, Entre-Deux-Mers—Bordeaux, France 2008; or any other Sauvignon Blanc

Menu:

- ◆ Arugula salad with citrus vinaigrette, toasted walnuts, and goat cheese
- ◆ Butternut squash ravioli with a brown butter sage sauce and toasted pine nuts
- ◆ Cheese plate of fresh chèvre, Brie, Havarti, aged cheddar, and Parmegiano-Reggiano served with rice crackers

Why it works: This simple meal has been created to pair with a Bordeaux white wine that is made up of primarily Sauvignon Blanc, plus some Semillon and Muscadelle. It is a crisp, dry, and aromatic wine with notes of herbs, citrus, and stone fruit. The herbaceous notes and acidity of the wine pair well with the arugula and vinaigrette, and the wine's intensity matches the intensity of the walnuts and goat cheese. The wine also pairs well with sage in the entrée and offers a contrast to the rich butter sauce. As for the dessert, it is a good idea to stick with something a little more savory since this wine is quite dry, so we went with a European-styled cheese plate.

Semi-Formal Home Party Featuring a Wine for Each Course

This wine menu shows how you can feature several wines with individual courses.

Salad with wine pairing:

- ◆ Spinach salad with strawberries and honey poppy seed vinaigrette
- ◆ Riesling, Chateau Ste. Michelle, Columbia Valley, Washington 2008

Soup with wine pairing:

◆ Mussel and fennel bisque

◆ Albariño, Martín Códax "Burgáns," Rias Baixas, Spain 2008

Entrée with wine pairing:

◆ Bacon-wrapped meatloaf with garlic mashed potatoes and baked carrots

◆ Shiraz, d'Arenberg "The Dead Arm," McLaren Vale, South Australia 2006

Dessert with wine pairing:

◆ Flourless chocolate cake

◆ Zinfandel Port, Meyer Family Cellars, Mendocino, California NV

Why it works: These pairings are arranged in an order that increases in intensity from each course to the next, allowing your palate to build up to the next level of intensity. (You always want to avoid having a lighter dish/wine follow a heavier dish/wine.) The spinach salad has a semi-sweet vinaigrette, and needs a slightly sweeter wine to go with it. The soup is highly aromatic with the addition of fennel and should be complimented with an equally aromatic wine. This crisp Albariño is also slightly fuller-bodied, so it matches well with the weight of the creamy soup. The meatloaf is paired with an equally intense Shiraz that is also known for its smoky, bacony aromas. And to finish it all off is a decadent and chocolate cake paired with an equally decadent Port.

Thanksgiving Dinner

Thanksgiving often presents a wine conundrum; here's an example of how you might want to pair this traditional meal.

Wines:

◆ Gewürztraminer, René Muré, Alsace, France 2007

◆ Gamay, Domaine Thivin, Côte de Brouilly—Beaujolais, France 2007

◆ Zinfandel, Seghesio, Sonoma, California 2008

Menu:

- ◆ Roasted turkey
- ◆ Mashed potatoes & gravy
- ◆ Herb and sausage stuffing
- ◆ Cranberry sauce
- ◆ Candied yams
- ◆ Buttery corn
- ◆ Green bean casserole
- ◆ Pumpkin pie

Why it works: Thanksgiving, and other large holiday meals, have a lot going on, so it is a great idea to offer a few different wines for everyone to enjoy interchangeably throughout the meal. An off-dry Gewürztraminer will compliment the turkey; work with the sweeter items like the corn, cranberry sauce, and yams; hold up to casseroles; and be delicious with dessert. Gewürztraminer has a ginger and cardamom-like spice note that will compliment the items on the table better than a Riesling. A cru Beaujolais will have a bit more structure to hold up to the gravy, but won't overpower the turkey. It will also pair delightfully with a less sweet cranberry sauce, as they both have similar aromas/flavors. It will also pair well with the herbs in the stuffing and add a nice contrast to the heaviness of the casseroles. Zinfandel is a nice wine to add to the mix if you have guests who like a heavy red wine. This all-American grape varietal fits with the theme, but it also works nicely with the spice in the sausage stuffing, and the intensity of the cranberry sauce.

One Bottle of Wine Paired with a Restaurant Dinner Menu for Two

This is an example of how you might select a bottle of wine at a restaurant to pair for two distinct dinners.

Restaurant: fianco, 3440 North Southport Avenue, Chicago, IL 60657 (www.fiancochicago.com); Executive Chef: Matt Troost

Wine:

- Michele Chiarlo, "Le Orme" Barbera d'Asti, Piedmont, Italy, 2006

Appetizers:

- Duroc pork belly with Sambuca glaze, sweet fennel jam, pickled fresno chili, Brussels sprout leaves

- House-made pâté with whole-grain mustard, house-made pickles, preserves and olive oil crackers

Salads:

- Grilled greens served with grilled pumpkin, brown-butter vinaigrette, walnuts, gorgonzola cheese

- Roasted tomato and taleggio tart, with frisee, bacon, chives, Sherry-walnut vinaigrette

Pasta:

- Hand-made black pepper pappardalle

- Wild boar Bolognese-style with parsley and pecorino cheese

Entrées:

- Duck meatballs with braised fennel, stewed tomato sauce, spoon polenta, parmesan cheese

- Bacon-wrapped pork tenderloin "porchetta style" with rosemary and toasted fennel rub, cider-braised cabbage, crispy leek spaetzle, and cider brown-butter sauce

Why it works: This menu illustrates how you can go to a restaurant with a friend, each order your own items from the regular dinner menu, and still find a way to pair the entire meal with one bottle of wine. After looking over the entire menu, we had to decide if we wanted to go with a bottle of red wine or a bottle of white wine. Since fianco serves many intense items in each course (even salads!), we felt that we could plan an entire meal that was intense enough to stand up to red wine. After consulting with each other on each course, we chose a variety of dishes that we believed would all share a similar intensity, while still providing a nice mix of ingredients and flavors. Since there are some lighter items, like the salads, and since we didn't go with the beef, we decided on a light-to-medium bodied red. Finally, since the meal contained a lot of aromatic herbs, spices, and earthy ingredients, we chose a wine that would embody the same notes in its aromatics. Barbera d'Asti is relatively light, yet intensely aromatic, making it perfect to share, and pair, with this entire meal.

Wine Dinner Menu Paired by Region

This is an example of a wine dinner prepared by a chef and designed for a specific geographical region.

Chef: Chef Thi Cao, of Milwaukee, WI

Soup with wine pairing:

- Parmesan soup (grated parmesan, parmesan cream, caramelized porcini, chive blossoms, extra-virgin olive oil drizzle)
- Tre Monti, Albana di Romagna, Emilia Romagna, Italy 2006

Entrée with wine pairing #1:

- Orecchiette and duck (duck confit, Chianti, mushrooms, fig vincotto)
- Badia a Coltibuono, Chianti Classico, Tuscany, Italy 2006

Entrée with wine pairing #2:

- Sea bass with vanilla-fennel served with orange segments
- Feudi di San Gregorio, Fiano di Avellino, Campania, Italy 2007

Entrée with wine pairing #3:

- Roast lamb loin with chorizo couscous, romesco sauce, and charred leeks
- La Valentina "Spelt," Montepulciano d'Abruzzo, Italy 2004

Dessert with wine pairing:

- Drunken torte (a bourbon-soaked pound cake) served with vanilla gelato and caramel sauce

- Isole e Olena, Vinsanto del Chianti Classico, Tuscany, Italy 2001

Why it works: Each course is paired with a wine that comes from where the most prominent ingredients of the dish originate. By using the "goes with where it grows" pairing concept, this wine dinner showcases lesser-known varietals from throughout Italy that are meant to go with the ingredients that inspired Chef Thi Cao to create each dish. The dessert, a unique creation with Italian flair, is paired with a fortified wine that could match the intensity of the bourbon-soaked cake.

Menu Featuring a Single Grape Varietal

Sometimes, a wine dinner highlights a single grape, and here is such an example, featuring (except for one course) all Pinot Noirs.

Restaurant: The Epicurean Connection, 18816 Sonoma Highway "C," Sonoma, CA 95476 (www.sheanadavis.com); Chef and Owner: Sheana Davis

Appetizers with wine pairings:

- Délice De la Vallée (a double-cream, fresh goat and cow's milk blended cheese)

- Chanterelles & hen-of-the-woods with white truffle oil crostini

- 2006 Hanzell Winery Estate Chardonnay

- 2006 David Noyes Russian River Pinot Noir

- 2006 Merry Edwards Sonoma Coast Pinot Noir

First course with wine pairings:

- Fall harvest, Oakhill Farm, fall salad with warmed hedgehog mushrooms, lobster mushrooms, and Yukon golden potatoes served with a chive blossom and Dijon mustard vinaigrette

- 2006 Hanzell Winery Estate Pinot Noir, Sonoma Valley

- 2006 Three Sticks Durell Vineyards Estate Reserve Pinot Noir, Sonoma Valley

Second course with wine pairings:

- Trumpet Royale & Velvet Pioppini mushrooms, crème fraiche bread pudding with Cannard Farms leeks, green garlic, and ruby-red swiss chard sprinkled with Vella dry jack cheese (a dry Monterey Jack cheese made in Sonoma County)

- 2005 Davis Family Vineyards Estate Pinot Noir, Sonoma County

- 2005 Parmelee Hill Estate Reserve Pinot Noir, Sonoma County

Third course with wine pairings:

- Wild mushroom polenta, including forest Nameko, clamshell alba, and clamshell amber mushrooms served with Pinot Noir–roasted Sonoma County lamb chop

- 2004 Parmelee Hill Estate Pinot Noir, Sonoma Valley

- 2004 Gloria Ferrer Estate Reserve Pinot Noir, Sonoma Valley

Dessert with wine pairings:

- Marble porcini mushroom cake served with crème de la crème fraiche and drizzled with a Pinot Noir reduction

- 2006 Nicholson Ranch Sonoma Valley/Napa Valley Blend Pinot Noir

Why it works: By choosing a theme, in this case only Pinot Noir wines, the chef is able to show off the versatility of the grape and how various pairings affect the wine. By utilizing the various aromas, earthy qualities, acidic structure, and lighter body, Chef Sheana was able to create numerous dishes that all, in their own special way, worked with various Pinot Noirs primarily from Sonoma. The Chardonnay at the beginning is a nice touch, though, because it offers your palate a bit of a jump-start before heading into all that Pinot.

Winemaker Dinner Featuring a Single Producer

Many wine dinners feature a single winemaker, and here's an example.

Restaurant: Jimtown Store, 6706 Hwy 128, Healdsburg, CA 95448 (www.jimtown.com); Winemaker: Jake Hawkes, Hawkes Winery, Alexander Valley, California; Executive Chef: Peter Brown

Amuse-bouche:

- Fresh pea soup with carrot and mint coulis

First course with wine pairing:

- Rock shrimp, asparagus, and preserved Meyer lemon risotto with mascarpone
- Hawkes, 2006 Chardonnay

Second course with wine pairing:

- Grilled grape leaves stuffed with spiced lamb, pine nuts, and currants
- Hawkes, 2004 Merlot

Third course with wine pairing:

- Lamb consommé with spring vegetables and fava beans
- Hawkes, 2002 Cabernet Sauvignon

Main course with wine pairing:

- Mixed grill of lamb with poached baby carrots and artichokes, hazelnut Romesco, potato and fennel gratin
- Hawkes, 2005 "Pyramid" Cabernet Sauvignon

Salad course:

- Baby lettuce with spring blossoms, toasted almonds, Dry Creek olive oil, and 25-year aged balsamic

Dessert with wine pairing:

- Lemon verbena pound cake with strawberries and late harvest Sabayon
- Hawkes, 2008 "Late Harvest" Sauvignon Blanc

Why it works: This menu was created to highlight the wines from a single producer from Alexander Valley, California. The dinner also features several different preparations for lamb, all of which are great with red wine. The Chardonnay's crispness and complexity is highlighted by its pairing, the Merlot's cinnamon-spice notes are intensified by the spiced lamb, the Cabernet's versatility and complexity is shown off by the grilled and nutty components of the dish, and the late harvest Sauvignon Blanc is harmoniously paired with the addition of the wine to the dish. It is also important to note that not every course was paired with wine. Typically, wine is not paired with the amuse-bouche because it is just a quick, small bite to start things off, not to sit and savor. And the salad course did not have a wine paired with it, likely because it was meant to show off the seasonal ingredients and act as an intermission between the courses.

Wine Dinner Featuring a Single Producer with a Dual-Paired Course

Restaurant: Riverbend Private Club at Destination Kohler, 1161 Lower Road, Kohler, WI 53044 (www.destinationkohler.com); Winemaker: Ehren Jordan, Failla Wines, Napa, CA; Executive Chef: Leonard "Lenny" Sorce; Beverage Manager: Teo Zagroba

Appetizer with wine pairing:

- Chef's selection of canapés
- Failla Viognier, "Alban Vineyard," Edna Valley 2007

First course with wine pairing:

- Seared sea scallop with smashed English peas, sautéed wild mushrooms, and minted yellow tomato relish
- Failla Chardonnay, "Keefer Ranch," Russian River Valley 2007

Second course with wine pairing:

- Pan-seared breast of quail with summer beans, sweet corn, black chickpeas, mustard sauce, and natural quail reduction

- Failla Chardonnay, "Keefer Ranch," Russian River Valley 2007

Third course with wine pairing:

- Crispy veal sweetbreads and seared Hudson Valley foie gras with braised strawberries, petite greens, and spiced strawberry almond vinaigrette

- Failla Pinot Noir, "Keefer Ranch," Russian River Valley 2007

Fourth course with wine pairing:

- Grilled rack of lamb with truffled goat cheese enhanced heirloom potato salad, glazed carrot pave, Syrah-braised cipollini onions, and natural lamb reduction

- Failla Pinot Noir, "Occidental Ridge," Sonoma Coast 2006

- Failla Syrah "Phoenix Ranch," Napa Valley 2007

Dessert course with wine pairing:

- Chocolate hazelnut-filled crespelle and dark chocolate doughnut

- Buttermilk blue cheese ice cream with black currant jam, and candied hazelnuts

- Failla Syrah, "Phoenix Ranch," Napa Valley 2007

Why it works: This wine dinner was held at Kohler's private club to feature the wines of Failla. Note how the same wine was used for multiple courses, and how two very different wines were showcased with the main course. These are great techniques to use when pairing at home. Chef Lenny developed this menu after tasting each wine and determining their unique flavor profiles. He then used individual aromas and characteristics to pair with specific ingredients, like matching the strawberry and spicy-nosed Pinot Noir with those exact ingredients in the third course. For the entrée, lamb was used since it is a versatile protein that works well with Pinot Noir and Syrah. This dual pairing gave attendees the chance to compare the impact each of the wines had on the dish. For dessert, a very creative dish was created to work with the dry Syrah. By using blue cheese, which matches the wine's intensity, plus chocolate and currants, which matches the wine's aromas, Chef Lenny was able to use Syrah as a "dessert" wine.

Wine Dinner Featuring Aged White Wines from a Single Region

This shows how a wine dinner can highlight a specific wine region.

Restaurant: Café Sebastienne at The Kemper Museum, 4420 Warwick Boulevard, Kansas City, MO 64111 (www.kemperart.org); Executive Chef: Jennifer Maloney

Hors d'oeuvres with wine pairing:

- Seared foie gras on crostini with rhubarb-apricot compote

- Onion tart

- Domaine Ostertag Riesling, "Vignoble D'Epfig" 1999

First course:

- Beet risotto with cambozola, lemon zest, and dill

Second course with wine pairing:

- Sautéed walleye with morels, baby green beans, fresh herbs, and cream

- Domaine Ostertag Pinot Gris, "Barriques" 1999

Third course with wine pairing:

- Roasted pork loin with summer vegetable gratin, braised red cabbage, and blueberry-mustard reduction

- Gustave Lorentz Reserve Pinot Gris 1999

Dessert with wine pairing:

- Cherry almond clafouti

- Dark French roast coffee

- Digestif of Pellegrino and limoncello

Why it works: This wine dinner shows the versatility, age-ability, and range of styles of Alsatian wines. Each of the courses is inspired by Alsatian dishes and ingredients, making great companions with the featured wines. Foie gras, onion tarts, and cabbage are all staples in Alsace. Those ingredients that aren't Alsatian in origin are paired by intensity and aroma/flavor. The second course highlights the Pinot Gris's aged bouquet with the inclusion of mushrooms and herbs, and the third course utilizes the increased intensity of the aged wine to pair it with pork and mustard. For dessert, diners were offered a choice of coffee and digestifs to help finish on an uplifted note.

Wine Dinner Organized to Showcase a Special Wine

Though many wines are featured in this dinner, the highlight of the dinner was the bottle of Caymus served with the second course.

Restaurant: Eagle Ridge Resort & Spa, 444 Eagle Ridge Drive, Galena, IL 61036 (www.eagleridgeresortonline.com); Executive Chef: Morgan Wesley; Sommelier: Steve Curtis; Director of Food and Beverage: Don Pleau

Appetizer with wine pairing:

- Veal sweetbreads with white bean, sage, and mustard seed flan; and spinach purée

- Domaine Cordier Viellies Vignes Pouilly Fuisse

Second course with wine pairing:

- Confit of tuna with pan-fried shiitake mushroom gnocchi, olive oil–poached tomatoes, Thai basil, and grilled Thai eggplant

- Caymus Vineyards 2005 Cabernet Sauvignon

Third course with wine pairing:

- Braised buffalo involtini with roasted root vegetables tossed with gremolata; and rosemary barley "risotto"
- Zenato Amarone della Valpolicella 2001

Dessert with wine pairing:

- Poached apple and walnut terrine with a fig and polenta fritter
- Markus Molitor Spätlese Riesling 2004

Why it works: This wine dinner was organized as part of a wine dinner series to highlight some of the sommelier's favorite wines. This particular dinner's showcase wine was Caymus Vineyards's Cabernet Sauvignon from Rutherford, California. The first wine, a Chardonnay from Burgundy, compliments the intensity of the sweetbreads, while also acting as an acidic counterbalance to the richness of the overall dish. The Cabernet Sauvignon is intuitively/experimentally paired with ahi tuna, which is usually overpowered by such a hearty red wine. But thanks to the addition of mushrooms and eggplant, both of which love tannic wines, this pairing works. The Valpolicella is matched by intensity and to the herbs in the third course. The final course finishes on a sweet note, with a Spätlese (sweeter-style) Riesling matched by intensity and sweetness to the dessert.

Chef's Degustation Menu Featuring Aged Rare and Collectable Wines

This wine dinner was designed by a chef for a special patron, who brought in his own collection of rare wines.

Restaurant: Restaurant EVE, 110 South Pitt Street, Alexandria, VA 22314 (www.restauranteve.com); Chef and Owner: Cathal Armstrong; General Manager and Sommelier: Todd Thrasher

First course with wine pairing:

- "OOO" (oysters, onions, and osetra caviar)
- Krug 1985

Second course with wine pairings:

- ◆ Terrine of Moulard foie gras with local fig jam
- ◆ 1989 Zind-Humbrecht Tokay-Pinot Gris Rangen de Thann Clos St. Urban "SGN"
- ◆ 1990 Merkelbach Riesling Auslese Urziger Wurzgarten Fuder #9

Third course with wine pairings:

- ◆ Fricassée of shellfish with leeks and baby potatoes
- ◆ 2000 Chave Hermitage
- ◆ 2000 Chapoutier Ermitage L'Orlee

Fourth course with wine pairing:

- ◆ Pan-roasted black sea bass with black truffles
- ◆ 1989 DRC Romanee Conti

Fifth course with wine pairings:

- ◆ Roasted pigeon with foie gras, honey caps, and red currants
- ◆ 1994 Araujo Cabernet
- ◆ 1994 Harlan Cabernet

Sixth course with wine pairings:

- ◆ A tasting of Vadon Farm's lamb
- ◆ 1982 La Mission Haut Brion
- ◆ 1982 La Tour Haut Brion

Seventh course with wine pairings:

- ◆ Cheese course
- ◆ 1988 Guigal Cotê Rotie "La Mouline"
- ◆ 1990 Jaboulet Hermitage "La Chapelle"

Dessert with wine pairing:

- ◆ Pineapple upside-down cake
- ◆ 1937 Caillou Barsac

Why it works: This is a great example of a very special dinner featuring very special wines from a patron's personal collection. This menu pulls out all the stops and pairs using all of the concepts covered in this book. Krug, a Champagne, is paired with caviar as a traditional pairing. Aged red wines are softer, yet increasingly complex, than their younger counterparts, making them better suited with seafood, poultry, and lamb. You'll also notice that the sommelier paired two different wines with some of the courses. These comparative pairings allow tasters to experience two wines that work with the same course, but they work in very different ways. You can replicate this type of menu at home by picking two wines to enjoy with the same course that are either from the same major region, made with the same grape from different regions or wineries, or by pairing two totally different wines that accent different ingredients in the dish.

Beer Dinner Menu Featuring Craft Beers from One Brewery

This is an example of pairing beers with courses instead of pairing wines.

Restaurant: Kil@wat at the Intercontinental Milwaukee, 139 East Kilbourn Avenue, Milwaukee, WI 53202 (www.kilawatcuisine.com); Executive Chef/Director of Food and Beverage: Robert Ash

Featured brewery: Lakefront Brewery—Milwaukee, WI

Appetizer with beer pairing:

- ◆ Cru of Labelle Farms duck and Growing Power chicken livers
- ◆ Elegant farmer apple salad, with bagel crisps, and Growing Power petite watercress
- ◆ Lakefront New Grist (gluten-free beer)

Salad with beer pairing:

- Grilled Maine lobster salad with Russian fingerling potatoes, chickory, Nueskes pork belly croute, haricot vert, and roasted piquillo vinaigrette

- Organic E.S.B. (extra special bitter)

Entrée with beer pairing:

- Strauss bone-in veal schnitzel with herb spaetzle, Brussels sprout leaves, caramelized Meyer lemon, and Pommery mustard-cream sauce

- Oktoberfest

Cheese course with beer pairing:

- Red Dragon Mustard Seed Cheese with Bavarian pretzel dust, and Door County cherry conserve

- Imperial stout

Dessert with beer pairing:

- Spiced pumpkin cremeux with gingerbread, pretzel, brandied caramel, candied orange-ginger gelato

- Pumpkin lager

Why it works: This dinner shows how you can apply wine-pairing principles to pairing beer. Each of the courses features local ingredients that are grown very close to where the beer is crafted, plus many of the courses are inspired by European dishes that are traditionally paired with beer, like pretzels and mustard. Each of the beers is paired by intensity with each course, and they are arranged from lightest to heaviest, giving the meal a nice progression. Additionally, the salad course is paired with a beer that boasts a hoppy bitterness as well as citrus components which compliment the salad. The dessert offers a "like with like" pairing by using the spices and flavors found in the beer, with ingredients in the dish like ginger and caramel.

Appendix E

Wine Pairing Resources

General References

Dornenburg, Andrew and Karen Page. *What to Drink with What You Eat*. New York: Bulfinch Press, 2006.

Church, Ruth Ellen. *Entertaining with Wine*. New York: Rand McNally & Company, 1976.

Smith, Jeff. *The Frugal Gourmet Cooks with Wine*. New York: William Morrow and Company, Inc, 1986.

Thomas, Tara Q. *The Complete Idiot's Guide to Wine Basics, Second Edition*. New York: Penguin Group, Inc, 2008.

Websites

Beer Cook
www.beercook.com

A guide to beer and beer pairings.

Bottega del Vino

www.bottegadelvinocrystal.com

A company that manufactures optical crystal wine glasses.

Bouquet the Wine Game

www.bouquetthewinegame.com

A fun way to learn more about wine.

Court of Master Sommeliers

www.mastersommeliers.org

An organization for wine certifications.

Epicurious

www.epicurious.com

A recipe database and foodie resource.

Great Lakes Distillery

www.greatlakesdistillery.com

An artisan distillery.

Larry's Market

www.larrysmarket.com

A specialty food market.

Life Between the Vines

http://lifebetweenthevines.com

Wine podcasts and blogs.

Mitsuwa Marketplace

www.mitsuwa.com

A specialty Japanese market.

Monica Bhide

www.monicabhide.com

Indian food expert.

Nat Decants

www.nataliemaclean.com/index.asp

Wine writer and guide.

Rishi Tea
www.rishi-tea.com

Gourmet tea company.

Sommelier Journal
www.sommelierjournal.com

Wine professional magazine.

Spice House
www.thespicehouse.com

Gourmet spice merchant.

Terroir France
www.terroir-france.com

Guide to French terroirs.

To Be a Snob
www.2basnob.com

Beverage-pairing guide.

Vinobite
www.vinobite.com

Blog with pairings, ratings, and recipes.

Wine and Music
www.wineandmusic.com

Wine and music pairing guide.

Wine Enthusiast
www.wineenthusiast.com

Wine magazine.

Wine Spectator
www.winespectator.com

Wine magazine.

Wines from Spain
www.winesfromspainusa.com

Guide to Spanish wines and terroirs.

Wine & Spirit Education Trust
www.wset.co.uk

Wine certification and educational foundation.

Wisconsin Cheese Cupid
www.cheesecupid.com

Cheese and beverage pairing guide.

Zingerman's Market
www.zingermans.com

Gourmet market.

Index

CHECK OUT THESE BEST-SELLERS

More than 450 titles available at booksellers and online retailers everywhere!

Grammar and Style
SECOND EDITION
978-1-59257-115-4

Word Search Puzzles
978-1-59257-900-6

Glycemic Index Weight Loss
SECOND EDITION
978-1-59257-855-9

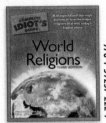
World Religions
THIRD EDITION
978-1-59257-222-9

U.S. HISTORY GRAPHIC ILLUSTRATED
978-1-59257-785-9

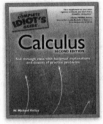
Calculus
SECOND EDITION
978-1-59257-471-1

Positive Dog Training
SECOND EDITION
978-1-59257-483-4

Personal Finance in Your 20s & 30s
FOURTH EDITION
978-1-59257-883-2

CD INCLUDED!
Learning Spanish
FIFTH EDITION
978-1-59257-908-2

Wine Basics
SECOND EDITION
978-1-59257-786-6

Microsoft Windows 7
978-1-59257-954-9

CD INCLUDED!
Music Theory
SECOND EDITION
978-1-59257-437-7

The Perfect Resume
FIFTH EDITION
978-1-59257-957-0

Organizing Your Life
FIFTH EDITION
978-1-59257-966-2

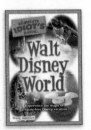
Walt Disney World
978-1-59257-888-7

ALPHA   idiotsguides.com